WINNING PLAYS

COUP D'ETAT: A farcical revolution in a "bananas" republic

SONATA: A child's mysterious disappearance has a startling effect on her parents

FIELD DAY: "War games" turn into a suicide mission for two young soldiers

THE GROUND ZERO CLUB: It's the meeting that every member of the Club has been waiting for: right on top of the Empire State Building, and right before a nuclear attack

WANING CRESCENT MOON: Two friends find a way to leave home—but not the past—behind

REMEDIAL ENGLISH: Vincent leads a life of fantasy, passion, and romance—in a Catholic boys' school?

These six plays by writers aged fifteen to eighteen were selected from the winners of the 1985 and 1986 Young Playwrights Festivals, a national contest. Each of these plays was given a professional production or reading at Playwrights Horizons, a theater in New York City.

The extraordinary variety of these remarkable plays—by turns hilarious, provocative, and moving—proves that the Festival is open to almost any kind of play. Any writer under the age of nineteen can enter the contest, and the Introduction here will tell you how. After all, reading these plays just might inspire *you* to write one of your own.

"Enormously entertaining."

—Howard Kissel, *Daily News* (New York)

"The Young Playwrights Festival is one of the few theatrical treats in town, and the young talents showcased deserve to be nurtured."

—Jacque le Sourd, *Gannett Westchester Newspapers*

Praise for
MEETING THE WINTER BIKE RIDER
and Other Prize-winning Plays from the 1983 and 1984 Young Playwrights Festivals

Edited by Wendy Lamb
Introduction by Gerald Chapman

An ALA Best Book for Young Adults

"This collection . . . presents a variety of material—dramatic, humorous, and satirical—which is entertaining to read and easily performed. But more important, this volume should serve as encouragement and inspiration to other talented young people. Statements from each author . . . indicate that gifted individuals, from whatever background, geographic area, or age group can be appreciated and rewarded."   —*School Library Journal*

"An exciting collection . . . the overall quality of the plays is excellent. You never say, 'A good play considering a 14-year-old wrote it.' Topics are varied, sophisticated, and well developed. While the plays are excellent entertainment, the short essays, introductions, and biographies of the playwrights are fascinating. Their descriptions of what participating in the Young Playwrights Festivals and winning meant to them, and how it affected their lives, are exciting and should inspire other young people to try to participate."

—*Voice of Youth Advocates*

The six plays in this anthology were selected from fifteen plays given full productions or staged readings in the Young Playwrights Festival in 1985 and 1986 at Playwrights Horizons in New York City. Produced by The Foundation of The Dramatists Guild, the Festival seeks to identify and encourage talented playwrights under the age of nineteen. Information about the Young Playwrights Festival is available at The Foundation of The Dramatists Guild, 234 West 44th Street, New York, New York 10036.

YOUNG PLAYWRIGHTS FESTIVAL STAFF

Peggy C. Hansen, Producing Director
Gerald Chapman, Education Director
Sheri M. Goldhirsch, Associate Director
Richard Wolcott, Program Coordinator

YOUNG PLAYWRIGHTS FESTIVAL COMMITTEE

Stephen Sondheim, Chairman
Andre Bishop
Christopher Durang
Jules Feiffer
Charles Fuller
Ruth Goetz
Micki Grant
A. R. Gurney, Jr.
Murray Horwitz
David E. LeVine
Eve Merriam
Mary Rodgers
Wendy Wasserstein

The Young Playwrights Festival is supported by numerous foundations, corporations, and individuals. In 1985 and 1986 major funding was provided by the Exxon Corporation, as well as by the Axe-Houghton Foundation, the Barker Welfare Foundation, CBS Inc., the Eleanor Naylor Dana Charitable Trust, Dollar Dry Dock, The Dramatists Guild Fund, the Jean and Louis Dreyfus Foundation, the Exxon Education Foundation, the Samuel Goldwyn Foundation, Stephen Graham, the George Link, Jr., Foundation, the Metropolitan Life Foundation, *New York Newsday,* the New York State Council on the Arts, the Richard and Dorothy Rodgers Foundation, the Shubert Foundation, and Wallace Funds. To all of the above and to our many other contributors, the Festival extends grateful appreciation.

From the 1985 and 1986
Young Playwrights Festivals
Produced by
The Foundation of
The Dramatists Guild

THE
GROUND ZERO
CLUB
and
Other Prize-winning
Plays

EDITED BY
Wendy Lamb
Introduction by Peggy C. Hansen

Published by
Dell Publishing Co., Inc.
1 Dag Hammarskjold Plaza
New York, New York 10017

PHOTO CREDITS:

Front cover:

Elizabeth Berridge as Angela, Larry Joshua as Sal, Polly
Draper as Feonna, and Tom Mardirosia as the Guard, in THE
GROUND ZERO CLUB, performed at Playwrights Horizons,
New York City, April 1985.
Copyright © 1985 by Susan Cook, Martha Swope Associates

Back cover:

Elizabeth Hirschhorn, Leslie Kaufman, Charlie Schulman,
Copyright © 1985 by Susan Cook, Martha Swope Associates
Stephen Serpas, Evan Smith, Copyright © 1986 by Susan
Cook, Martha Swope Associates
Carolyn Jones, Copyright © 1986 by John Covello

Printed in the United States of America
October 1987
10 9 8 7 6 5 4 3 2 1
OPM

CONTENTS

INTRODUCTION

The plays in this anthology were written by six young people between the ages of fifteen and eighteen. They were all given professional productions or readings as part of the 1985 and 1986 seasons of the Young Playwrights Festival at Playwrights Horizons in New York City. A project of The Foundation of The Dramatists Guild, Inc., the Festival aims to identify and encourage talented playwrights under the age of nineteen.

The Foundation of The Dramatists Guild was formed six years ago by members of The Dramatists Guild, the professional organization of playwrights, composers, and lyricists in the United States. In 1981, members of this organization decided to form a new group to sponsor projects of special interests to dramatists. The Foundation's first project was the Young Playwrights Festival.

Each year, about 700 young writers submit plays to the Festival. Each play is carefully evaluated by a preliminary reader, and a written report is sent to the playwright. About twenty-five plays are chosen to be read by the full Young Playwrights Festival Committee (Andre Bishop, Christopher Durang, Jules Feiffer, Charles Fuller, Ruth Goetz, Micki Grant, A. R. Gurney, Jr., Murray Horwitz, Eve Merriam, Mary Rodgers, Stephen Sondheim, and Wendy Wasserstein). The committee then selects approximately ten semifinalist plays, which are given readings with professional actors and directors. The semifinalist playwrights are brought to New York—all expenses paid!—to attend the readings and meet the committee. Then the committee makes its final selection of plays for the Festival season. Usually, three or four plays receive full productions in one full-length program; another three to six plays are given staged readings. Once again, the playwrights are brought to New York and spend about two months participating in casting, design meetings, rehearsals, and previews.

Because in most cases the Festival marks a young person's first contact with the professional theater, we try to represent the profession at its best. The professional theater is a community, and like all communities, it depends for its survival on being able to pass on its values to a new generation. We communicate our passion for the theater by bringing together some of its "leading lights"—directors, actors, designers, stage managers, technicians—who contribute their own special talents to each play in the Festival. The high standard of production makes several statements:

- the work is worth taking seriously
- the theater itself is serious about attracting new writers
- the theater can provide a forum for the ideas of young writers and therefore should command the serious attention of young audiences.

Ron Lagomarsino, director of *Remedial English* in the 1986 Festival, was interviewed toward the end of rehearsals and asked what it was like to work with an eighteen-year-old playwright. He said, "The most unusual thing about the project is that it hasn't been unusual at all." When I heard this, I knew we were doing something right. We want the Festival experience to be indistinguishable from that of *any* writer's first professional production.

This philosophy brings with it certain disadvantages. We do not protect our writers. The plays are reviewed by the New York press, and while Festival reviews have been generally very favorable, there have been exceptions, and a few specific comments have been genuinely unkind. During our rehearsals, just as in any other rehearsals, the writer is exposed to a full range of experiences—exhilarating, deeply satisfying, upsetting, frustrating. When the set change is too long, or the sound system isn't working, or the actor threatens to quit, or the director wants a bit of staging the playwright doesn't like—this, too, is the stuff of theater, and we make no attempt to screen it out.

We do try to support the playwrights as best we can. We give them dramaturgs, usually professional playwrights, who serve as guides to the rehearsal process. The Festival committee itself is a support. Knowing that one's play was selected by this country's leading dramatists bolsters confidence and can smooth some of the bumps along the way. But ultimately the theatrical event itself almost always transcends whatever came before. When the house lights go down and the audience's anticipation rises as they turn their attention to the stage, where the actors begin to perform *your play*—what else exists, what else matters?

The plays in this book display a full range of styles and concerns. *The Ground Zero Club, Field Day,* and *Sonata* were among nine plays presented in the 1985 Festival. While many Young Playwrights Festival plays explore personal experiences, these particular plays have a considerably larger and more public focus. *Field Day,* it seems to me, examines the power of the individual and the dignity inherent in the refusal, however absurd, to go along with arbitrary authority. All of the events in the play bring the characters face to face with the absurd: there is nothing sensible they can do in their situation. Although the subject is deadly serious, the play handles it with a light touch. In *Field Day,* an irresistible force meets an immovable object; both sides are equally committed to actions that make no sense.

In rehearsal, *Field Day* almost took a wrong turn that threatened this absurd spirit. Halfway through the rehearsal period, the playwright, at the suggestion of her dramaturg, made a very small adjustment. Rather than beginning the play with Man #1 having decided not to go on the mission, this decision became the action of the play. What happened during the play *caused* Man #1 to decide not to go. Although only two or three lines were changed, within the space of three rehearsals we were looking at an entirely different play! The absurdity, the humor, the metaphor were gone; we were suddenly watching a naturalistic play about a soldier making a decision in wartime. A conference was called; we agreed that we were heading in the wrong direction, and the original text was restored.

The Ground Zero Club, although entirely different in form, is also rooted in an appreciation of the absurd. On one level, the play taps in to the humor we all use to defend ourselves against the unthinkable—in this case a nuclear attack on New York City. On another, through the odd collection of characters who inhabit this play, the writer identifies a number of specific absurdities: Sal's belief in the existence of the Ground Zero Club; Bob's hypocritical and short-lived contrition; Feonna's boredom and jadedness; Angela's pathetic hope that Sal will someday "straighten out." It is as if the impending doom brings out each character's need to find some meaning in his life—and this only serves to underline the play's satiric point.

In production, the play went through a crisis common to many comedies—terrible final dress rehearsals where everyone is sure *it's not funny.* Maybe because the "audience" was composed of Festival personnel who had seen too many rehearsals, or because the actors were trying too hard, or because a long period of technical rehearsals had slowed the pace—for whatever reason, everything fell flat. We had to go on faith: it had been funny before; it would be funny again! A few nights later, in front of a *real* audience dissolved in laughter, we all breathed a lot easier!

Sonata, like the other two plays from the 1985 season published here, concerns itself with a public event, in this case the disappearance of a child and its effect both on the parents and on the detective who leads the investigation. More profoundly, the play suggests that even the most terrible losses often bring with them some gain. The parents, despite their grief, gain more time for themselves and each other, as well as a tremendous amount of sympathy and attention. To me, it is a startling observation—unsentimental and relentlessly honest. The play was extremely controversial, angering many people who saw it, while impressing others.

We got some idea about the level of difficulty in *Sonata* early in auditions. We saw dozens of fine actors, but no one found the right style. They were too mannered, or they were too naturalistic; it all suddenly became a soap opera, then a grade-B movie, then a drawing-room comedy. Wrong! We had to delay the first rehearsal and extend the auditions. Finally, we found the right company; rehearsals began. To find and sustain that style was the challenge of the next four weeks. The director struggled to define it. The playwright, for her part, came in with a major new rewrite almost every day. By the time the Festival opened, we had located the special world of this play—a delicate border between fantasy and reality. The parents seemed like the nice couple next door, yet the play's lyric rhythms never felt out of place.

The other three plays in this volume were selected from the six plays presented in the 1986 Young Playwrights Festival. *Coup d'Etat* shares the more public focus of the 1985 plays, while *Waning Crescent Moon* and *Remedial English* have more personal stories to tell. *Coup d'Etat*'s comic vision reveals a world—the rebellious island of St. Passis—where chaos reigns, the powerful behave like children, and idealism quickly succumbs to the lure of personal profit. The secret bewilderment with which most Americans greet news of coups and countercoups in countries with histories so complicated that only a small number really understand them is one of the most delightful and subtle subjects of the play's satire.

Partly for this reason, the director decided early in production that we would treat *Coup d'Etat* not as a politically sophisticated and knowing satire but as a broad comedy with Marx Brothers–like overtones. For example, the throne was on wheels and was fashioned entirely out of materials from cars—complete with bucket seat, tire rims, spoked wheels, horn, clip-on fan, headlights, and gearshift! Much of the comic business involved characters being wheeled around the huge conference table, on which was painted a map of the world, with the tiny island of St. Passis located smack in its center.

Waning Crescent Moon, which received a staged reading in the 1986 Festival, concerns itself with the coming of age of two teenage boys. To me, it captures in moving detail that painful and heady time when a young person realizes he must create his own life—that he is no longer defined by his history with his parents.

Now in its fifth draft, this script has undergone extensive revisions since it was first submitted to the Festival. The changes, which I think strengthened the play, have been in the direction of clarifying the nature of Scooter's disorder, lightening the moon symbolism, and making the relationship between Scooter and Hal more active and dynamic. This is a complex play with a lovely, lyrical quality and a real sense of truth.

Remedial English also underwent major revisions during the Festival process. A candid depiction of a day in the life of a bright, homosexual teenager at a Catholic boys' school, this play totally disarms us with its unselfconscious honesty, its wit, and its charm. Although these qualities were present from its earliest draft, the revisions served to tighten the play's focus and to keep its action moving along smoothly. This was accomplished at the sacrifice of some wonderful lines of dialogue; in some cases even entire pages or scenes had to go. The playwright displayed a remarkable ability to keep his eye on what best served his play.

One of the interesting stories about *Remedial English* is that when we went into rehearsal it had no ending. The playwright tried several approaches. After Rob's exit, Vincent simply looked at the audience with a wry smile; Rob reentered for a short final scene; Vincent had a final encounter with Sister Beatrice; and, one at a time, a number of poems were used in an attempt to end the play. The Dorothy Parker poem "Comment" was not selected until five days before the first preview. And that's when the real nail-biting began, because we still had to obtain the rights to use it! In a true theatrical cliffhanger, permission was phoned in to The Foundation of The Dramatists Guild's office six hours before the play had its first public performance. Of course we had chosen an alternative ending in case permission was not obtained, but no one liked it very much—and so the phone call triggered great jubilation among playwright, director, producer, company, and crew.

If these backstage stories or the plays in this book stimulate your interest in writing a play, I have one major piece of advice: *Do it!* We're waiting to hear from you. The great majority of plays we present in the Festival are first plays, many of them written by young people who started out thinking "I can't" or "I don't know how." Take out some paper and make a commitment to write one scene; then see where that takes you. Although only a few plays each year are selected for the Festival, *every* entrant receives a detailed written report on his or her script.

The deadline for submissions is October 1; playwrights must be under the age of nineteen on the previous July 1 (three months before the deadline). Plays should be typed and bound, with the author's name, address, home phone number, and date of birth on the title page. Scripts should be sent to the Young Playwrights Festival, The Foundation of The Dramatists Guild, 234 West 44th Street, New York, New York 10036.

I will conclude with a word of thanks to our many funding sources and contributors (see partial listing at front), to Playwrights Horizons theater management and staff, and to the hundreds of actors, directors, dramaturgs, readers, workshop leaders, designers, stage managers, and technicians who have made the Young Playwrights Festival a very special and successful event. A final thank you goes to every young writer who sits down and writes a play. Without that act of daring and determination, the Festival would not exist.

—PEGGY C. HANSEN
Producing Director

COUP D'ETAT

BY CAROLYN JONES
(age eighteen when play was written)
San Rafael, California

NOTE:
For the purpose of publication in this collection, certain words
have been changed by the playwright, and some profanity has
been deleted from the working script of the play as performed at
Playwrights Horizons, New York City, September 16 through
October 12, 1986.

CHARACTERS

CHILDREN
MAMA
JUAN
PAPA
KING
ABDUL
ENRICO
STEPHANIE
YURI BRUSHNIK
TROY LeFLAME
JULIO FERNANDEZ

SCENE ONE

The curtain opens as the poor family of the Caribbean island St. Passis is sitting down to dinner. There are about thirteen children running around the room, making a mess, and breaking things. Some are lying down. In the middle of the room is a large vat filled with beans. There are also a few chickens. The eldest son, JUAN, *is helping his mother set the table. They are obviously disturbed about something.*

(Enter PAPA.*)*

CHILDREN: Papa! Papa!

PAPA: Hello, kiddies!

MAMA: Carlos!

PAPA: What's the matter?

MAMA: Haven't you heard?

PAPA: Heard what?

CHILD: Look what I made, Papa!

JUAN: Papa, there's been another revolution. The revolutionaries have been overthrown.

MAMA: There've been riots everywhere. Rosie's husband was executed this morning. Hundreds more died just in our community!

JUAN: All of St. Passis is in chaos and disorder!

PAPA: I didn't hear of it. Are you sure? What happened?

JUAN: The rebels were overthrown this morning by the contra

army. The entire government was executed. Thousands more will die or lose their jobs.

MAMA: It's terrible, terrible!

PAPA: Who will die or lose their jobs?

JUAN: Anyone associated with the revolutionary movement.

PAPA: Oh, no! My boss just enlisted in the rebel army last week! No wonder he didn't show up for work this morning! I'm out of a job now.

MAMA *(beginning to cry):* What will we do? We're nearly starving on what you bring home now! And little Ramona has the fever. . . . How will we care for her? And what about Jose's broken collarbone?

CHILDREN *(whining):* I'm hungry. . . . I don't feel good. . . . Mama, I'm cold. . . . Papa, I feel sick. . . .

PAPA: Now, children.

MAMA: Oh, my babies. My poor, hungry, sick babies. What's to become of us?

JUAN *(suddenly jumping downstage):* Don't worry, Mama and Papa! I'll save this family! I'll make sure we have enough food to eat and enough shelter and enough medicine and none of us are endangered by the new government and—

PAPA: Juan, sit down. You're getting hysterical.

MAMA: Juan, how could you help us? You're just a boy!

PAPA: Maria, he's twenty-five.

MAMA: Yes, but he's very immature for his age.

PAPA: Are you going to get a job, Juan? Are you going to work?

JUAN: Don't be ridiculous. I'm going to the capital.

MAMA: Where?

PAPA: Why would you want to go to Fordtown this time of year? It's so humid. And these riots? You could be hurt!

JUAN: I must do everything I can to stop the evil government from harming not only us but all the proletariat! I must save all the peasants from the destruction which lies ahead! Together we will rise up and overthrow the oligarchy!

PAPA: Couldn't you just get a job, like other boys your age?

CHILD: Juan, what's that on your chin?

JUAN: Mama, Papa, I'd like to thank you for raising me. Good-bye, siblings. Don't fight too much, and be obedient for Mama and Papa. Good-bye, chickens, good-bye, bean vat. Good-bye, family. I'm off to Fordtown! Farewell!

MAMA *(sobbing):* Juan! My baby!

PAPA: Juan, you forgot your sombrero!

SCENE TWO

A luxurious office with a view of downtown Fordtown. There is a large, oval table in the middle, chairs, a throne, and a few pictures on the wall. The KING, ABDUL, *and* ENRICO *enter.*

KING: Ah! It's good to be back!

ENRICO: The table is dusty. I am allergic to dust.

ABDUL: I left my book in here somewhere. . . .

KING: It's been ages since I sat in my throne!

ENRICO: It was only last week.

KING: Seems like ages.

ABDUL: Ah! Here it is!

KING: What book is that, Abdul?

ABDUL: It is called *Southern California Sins*. It is very good. It is about a woman named Belinda who is a lifeguard by day and by night a—

ENRICO: Your Majesty, we have work to do.

KING: Of course we do. Get Stephanie.

ENRICO: It's her lunch hour.

ABDUL: You only have one secretary? I had ten or twelve.

KING: She's good, though. As good as ten or twelve.

ENRICO: We have to reorganize our government.

KING: Of course we do. We don't want to have what happened last week happen again, do we? That Guadalupe Motel 6 was not pleasant at all.

ABDUL: Certainly not. It was horrible.

ENRICO: Unless we do it now, there may be another revolution.

KING: Well, quick! Let's do something!

ABDUL: I vote for absolute monarchy.

KING: That's my vote, too.

ENRICO: We can't do that because there'll be another revolution.

KING: If you're so smart, then, what should we do, Enrico?

ENRICO: I suggest we become a limited monarchy.

(Long pause.)

ABDUL: What is he saying?

KING: I don't know. He gets like this sometimes. What are you talking about?

ENRICO: We just have to have a Parliament or something. It's really no big deal. England has one, and it's working out quite nicely.

ABDUL: I wouldn't trust him.

ENRICO: Will you stay out of this?

KING: Abdul is my friend.

ENRICO: All he does is interfere.

KING: He's our adviser. You don't interfere, do you, Abdul?

ABDUL: Nope.

(Enter STEPHANIE.*)*

STEPHANIE: What are you doing here? I thought you were overthrown.

KING: Hello, Stephanie.

ENRICO: Our army overthrew the revolutionaries, so we're back again.

STEPHANIE: Well, things had better be a little more stable around here, or I'm quitting, Your Highness. I mean, I just can't deal with all this chaos. Did you see those hippies who were in here last week? It was absolutely out of control. They broke the intercom—

ABDUL: Is this your secretary?

STEPHANIE: *You're* still here?

ABDUL: Have her flogged.

STEPHANIE: What?!

ABDUL: How do you allow such disrespectful women to work for you?

STEPHANIE: You were supposed to have been shot last week.

ABDUL: Your Majesty, she would not survive one day in my country.

STEPHANIE: And we all know how socially advanced your country is. Are women still sporting those black veils? Lots of detached right hands lying around? How many wives are you up to now?

ABDUL: She is intolerable! Where did she come from?

KING: I ordered her from Kelly Girls. I like her very much, though. She's very good at the typewriter.

STEPHANIE: Speaking of typewriters, Your Highness, do you realize that we're the only Third World government that doesn't own one word processor? Patty over on St. Thomas not only has her own PC, but she tells me the paperwork for the entire administration is on one floppy disk! I'm too embarrassed to tell her we're still using manual typewriters and Pee Chee folders.

ENRICO: Stephanie, you give me a headache.

KING: Stephanie, will you take notes on this conversation? We're talking about getting a new government.

STEPHANIE: Oh. Well, will it take long?

ABDUL: No. We're getting a new monarchy.

KING: Okay.

ENRICO: Let's not make any rash decisions.

ABDUL: Do you have any other suggestions? Besides your "limited" monarchy?

ENRICO: There's lots of other governments. We could pick anything. Fascism, democracy, anarchy—

KING: I like what we have now.

ENRICO: No one else does, though. We're not too popular at the UN, and our people think we're cruel and unfair and—

ABDUL: What's cruel and unfair?

ENRICO: Oh, you know. The 75 percent income tax, the two-thirds unemployment rate, the inflation. They don't like the justice system or the closed borders—

KING: I didn't know we had a justice system.

ABDUL: I don't know what the people are complaining about. They live on the most beautiful island in the whole Caribbean! Good weather, lots of beaches. And look what we have! A 360-day-a-year vacation, great food, wealth, power, palaces—we can't give all that up *now*.

KING: That's true.

STEPHANIE: Listen. What you need isn't a new government but a good public relations man.

ENRICO: Don't be silly.

STEPHANIE: No, really. I know a guy in Florida who can do wonders. Your image will improve, and you won't have to change a thing.

KING: That sounds like a good idea.

ABDUL: Are you sure?

STEPHANIE: I'll call him right now. His name is Troy LeFlame. We went to Tampa State together.

(As STEPHANIE exits, YURI BRUSHNIK enters.)
Excuse me, do you have an appointment?

BRUSHNIK: I don't need one. Good afternoon. My name is Yuri Brushnik.

ENRICO: Who are you?

BRUSHNIK: I am an adviser from the Soviet Union. We heard that you were in the market for a new government.

ENRICO: Yes, that's right.

ABDUL: Say, I like your tie.

BRUSHNIK: Thank you. Have you any ideas of what you want? Left, right, middle of the road?

KING: Whatever absolute monarchy is. Right, I guess.

BRUSHNIK: You're kidding, right? Not a real monarchy!

KING: Yes. What's wrong with that?

BRUSHNIK: Well, they're not exactly the most fashionable government these days. I mean, real monarchies! Tell me, which one of you is the king? No wait, let me guess.

KING: I am the king.

BRUSHNIK: So you are. I should've known by the crown. Are those real jewels?

KING: Don't touch. *(Slaps* YURI's *hand.)*

ENRICO: Can we get to the point?

BRUSHNIK: Of course. *(Opens briefcase, laughing to himself.)* Gromyko wasn't kidding. Okay. Now. I understand that you need a new government as soon as possible. I assume you want one in which you can retain most of your power.

ABDUL: And wealth.

BRUSHNIK: That, too.

ENRICO: That's true.

KING: That's right.

BRUSHNIK: Have you considered communism? Now, I know what you're thinking. You're saying to yourself, "Better Dead than Red." Well, did you know that half the world's population is Communist? Unbelievable, isn't it?

KING: Really? Half the world?

ABDUL: Don't trust him. I've dealt with these fellows before. They're tricky.

BRUSHNIK: Don't be so skeptical, my little OPEC friend. You have much to look forward to in dealing with my country.

ENRICO: Go on.

BRUSHNIK: We can send in advisers to help you get started, and if you need them, troops. *(Shows pictures of advisers and troops.)* It may take a while, but in the long run, I'm sure you'll agree it's worth it. Look at Albania *(shows picture)*, Czechoslovakia *(shows picture)*, East Germany *(on reverse of Albania)*—all prosperous. And I can guarantee you a deluge of gold medals at the next Olympics. *(Hands gold medal to KING.)*

KING: Well, I don't know.

ABDUL: No. We won't take it. Go back to Cuba.

BRUSHNIK: I've got some brochures here for you, and a lovely slide presentation. *(Hands brochures around; gives KING ViewMaster.)* If you have any questions—

(Enter STEPHANIE.)

STEPHANIE: Sorry to interrupt, but the most amazing thing just happened. I talked to Troy's mother, and she said Troy is right here on St. Passis! So I called his hotel—he's here on vacation— and he said he'd be right over. Isn't that marvelous?

KING: Marvelous.

(Enter TROY with piña colada.)

TROY: Howdy.

STEPHANIE: Troy! So good to see you!

TROY: Stephanie, you look great!

STEPHANIE: Glad you could make it on such short notice. This is Enrico, the prime minister, this is the king, this is his friend Abdul, and this is Yuri something. *(They all shake hands.)* It's all yours, Troy.

TROY: So, you need a new rep. Reputation.

ENRICO: Yes, we think so.

ABDUL: If we don't do something soon, there'll be another revolution.

TROY: Ouch. Me being the kind of fella I am, I like to get the whole picture: That's just the way I am. So could you tell me a little—

KING: I am a monarch.

TROY: I see. A king, right?

BRUSHNIK: Who are you? Where did you come from? What's going on?

TROY: Hey, dial down, gramps. I'm a public relations artist from Tampa. Who are you?

BRUSHNIK: Did George Shultz send you?

TROY: George who?

BRUSHNIK: Ah! It's perfect! The ideal conspiracy! What a cover-up!

TROY: What is he talking about?

BRUSHNIK: Nothing. Go on. I want to hear this. *(Quickly snaps a picture of TROY.)*

TROY: Whatever. On the way over I made a brief list of suggestions, just for starters. Do you want to hear it? *(The suggestions are scribbled on a cocktail napkin.)* The first thing you have to do is change the name of your capital city. You're going to be in the news a lot from now on, and I don't want to be rude or anything —that's not the kinda guy I am—but Fordtown just doesn't cut the mustard—if you know what I mean, and I think you do.

KING: But Gerald is our friend!

ABDUL: We can't hurt his feelings!

ENRICO: What do you suggest, then?

TROY: Reaganberg. *(Everyone laughs.)* It's not funny. A lot of people like him.

ABDUL: What else is on your list?

TROY: You should absolutely get an international airport. And an indoor shopping mall downtown somewhere. I think you should get Club Med to come in and take over half the beaches, build condos on the rest, and open a giant amusement park between here and the coast. Your newspaper, *The Fordtown Funnies,* has gotta go. I mean, I like the comics, too, but what happens when *60 Minutes* comes down here for a visit? You need something a little more, you know, mature. How about *The Reaganberg Daily Rap?* Or something. You'll need some prefab in the suburbs. You have suburbs, don't you? Or at least a trailer park? Video rental stores, McDonald's, cable TV, tanning clinics—and what else? Oh, a pro football team would be great. And a frozen yogurt chain.

ENRICO: But we only have eighty thousand people on the island.

TROY: No prob. Just have a baby boom.

BRUSHNIK: How decadent! Shultz is a genius.

TROY: And a national anthem. I, being kinda musical, suggest that you change the words to "Yellow Submarine," a song everybody knows already. Something like "We all live on the isle of St. Passis, the isle of St. Passis, the isle of St. Passis . . ."

(Everybody sings and starts dancing. STEPHANIE *exits to get a Tab.)*

ENRICO: But would we lose any power?

TROY: Nope. Might even gain some.

ENRICO: Hmmm. . . . It sounds good.

KING: I like it, especially the amusement park.

TROY: We could even get *People* magazine down here for an in-depth travel analysis. The population should boom after that.

ABDUL: I like it. We'll take it. How much will it cost?

TROY: A-hem. My fee, see, is—

BRUSHNIK *(banging shoe on table):* Wait a minute! You can't be serious?

ABDUL: Of course I'm—*we're* serious.

ENRICO: Abdul is interfering again.

TROY: Should I just bill you?

ABDUL: Yes. Here's our card.

KING: I don't know how much money we have in our account. Do you, Enrico?

ENRICO: Stephanie does.

ABDUL: Stephanie!

(Enter STEPHANIE *with a Tab.)*

KING: How much money do we have?

STEPHANIE: Let's see. *(Gets out personal checkbook.)* The hippie revolutionaries ran up an incredible deficit. The United States offered to send them weapons, but they wanted cash instead. Small, unmarked bills.

BRUSHNIK: See? The United States is your enemy. Did they send *you* any weapons?

KING: Well, no . . .

BRUSHNIK: We would send you anything you wanted.

ENRICO: What did the revolutionaries do with the money?

ABDUL: How much was it?

STEPHANIE: About ten million or so. They had a lot of parties, they bought a new Xerox machine, a blender, a CD player— which they took with them. They paid some old debts, stuff like that. Julio and I—I mean, Julio Fernandez went to Barbados for a few days. They invested a lot of it. I think some of them went to Las Vegas. So we have a grand total of . . . two dollars and forty-three cents left.

ENRICO: They spent $9,999,997.57 in one week?

ABDUL: Even I couldn't do that.

STEPHANIE: They didn't spend all of it. When you overthrew them, they still had about eight million dollars left. I don't know what happened to it. It's not in this account.

ENRICO: If we locate that eight million, we can pay Troy and remodel our country.

TROY: Hey, coincidentally, my fee—plus construction and overhead—is just under eight million! If you start right away, you can be ready to go by next summer.

KING: Let's start right away then!

BRUSHNIK: And if you can't locate that money? You certainly won't be able to afford your expensive public relations stunt.

ENRICO: We'd have to go with your idea.

ABDUL: I'd leave. I refuse to live in a communist country.

STEPHANIE: Promise?

BRUSHNIK: I have your word, then, that if you can't afford Mr. LeFlame's public relations idea, you will accept our advisers and begin implementing communism?

KING: Oh, I guess so. As long as we still have as much power. It's been in my family since 1979, you know.

BRUSHNIK: Will you sign here? We'll give you one week to find that money. I think that's fair.

ABDUL: It's a mistake, Your Majesty. Don't do it.

KING: What do you think, Enrico?

ENRICO: Sign, Your Highness. We'll be committing political suicide if you don't.

KING: Political suicide? *(He shrugs and signs an X.)*

BRUSHNIK: There. Fine. Just fine.

KING: Tell me, why are you so eager to sell us communism?

BRUSHNIK: I get paid on commission.

TROY: Hey, Steph, do you know what the revolutionaries did with that money? The eight big ones?

STEPHANIE: I have no idea. Someone must have it, though. I mean, eight million just doesn't disappear.

ENRICO: Most of the revolutionaries were executed.

ABDUL: We don't even know where to begin to look. This could take forever. I wish my citizenship wasn't revoked in my homeland. Then I could write us a check.

TROY: Why was your citizenship revoked?

ABDUL: I had a spat with His Royal Highness.

STEPHANIE: He was arrested for tax evasion, forgery, and fraud.

ENRICO: We must begin the search somewhere. Do you have any suggestions?

KING: If only we had someone to lead us to it!

(Enter JUAN, very dramatically.)

JUAN: Hah! There you are, you scum monarchs! You won't get away with oppressing the people anymore, because we won't stand for it!

ENRICO: Who are you?

JUAN: I'm unofficially representing all the proletariat, and we're going to rise up and overthrow you pigs!

ABDUL: Ah! Have a seat. What did you say your name was?

JUAN: Juan.

KING: Hello, Juan.

ENRICO: Juan, tell me. You're a revolutionary?

JUAN: Well, yes.

ABDUL: So glad you dropped by.

ENRICO: Let's chat awhile.

STEPHANIE: Juan, I love that adorable hat.

ABDUL: Do you know any of the other revolutionaries? The ones who took over last week?

JUAN: Not personally, no. I've heard of them, though.

ENRICO: You know their names?

JUAN: Sure. Luis Rodriguez, Diego Gomez, Raphael Goldstein—

STEPHANIE: Oh—don't remind me. The biggest slobs you've ever seen. Dirty ashtrays, laundry on the floor, cigarette butts—

ABDUL: They had eight million dollars when they were arrested. They were all hanged, though, except that one who escaped. What's his name? You know, the guy with the nervous twitch.

JUAN: Julio Fernandez.

ABDUL: Right.

ENRICO: So do you know where the money is?

JUAN: I think so.

ABDUL *and* ENRICO: Where?

JUAN *(coming to his senses):* Why should I tell you?

ABDUL: We'll give you the ambassadorship to any country you want if you tell us.

JUAN: Okay. I like Italian food a lot.

BRUSHNIK: Wait a minute. Juan, I'd like to speak to you privately. May I?

ABDUL: No, he's our guest.

BRUSHNIK *(walking downstage with* JUAN*)*: Juan, exactly how involved were you in last week's coup?

JUAN: Oh, I stuffed envelopes, walked precincts, answered the phone—stuff like that.

KING *(reading* Southern California Sins*)*: Shhhhh . . .

BRUSHNIK: I see. Did you ever have contact with the three men you mentioned earlier?

JUAN: I saw Diego Gomez's speech at the opening of the new K mart in my neighborhood. He was very inspiring.

BRUSHNIK: So you have no idea where the money is.

JUAN: The eight million dollars?

BRUSHNIK: Yes.

JUAN: To be honest, I—can I trust you?

BRUSHNIK: Of course.

JUAN: Well, I didn't even know they had money. If I did, I would've joined their forces a lot sooner. I'm broke, see. So is my poor family back home. We have not enough food on the table at night. Nearly all my thirteen brothers and sisters are ill. My father is unemployed—

BRUSHNIK *(preoccupied):* Good, good. You can go sit down now.

ABDUL *(to* JUAN*):* What did he say? Was he rude?

KING: Stephanie, get me a lemonade.

ENRICO: I'll have a Scotch.

STEPHANIE: Who do you think I am?

ENRICO: Do it anyway. I'll promote you.

STEPHANIE: You're as bad as Abdul.

ABDUL: I wouldn't promote you.

KING: Stephanie, I'm thirsty.

JUAN: Can I trust you?

ABDUL: Of course.

JUAN: Well, I forgot his name, but—

BRUSHNIK: Brushnik. Yuri Brushnik.

JUAN: Yuri asked me if I really knew where the money is.

ENRICO: You're not supposed to ask him that!

BRUSHNIK: Shut up.

JUAN: It's okay. I don't know where it is, anyway.

ABDUL *(after a pause):* Can you guess?

ENRICO: This is ridiculous.

BRUSHNIK: Now what are you going to do?

TROY: Listen. I can lower my rates, and you can probably get some big American corporation to donate the rest and write it off their taxes.

(Enter STEPHANIE with drinks.)

STEPHANIE: Guess who took the Scotch with them. We only have Hawaiian Punch.

KING: Thank you. *(Puts book down.)* Now, what is all this you're talking about?

ENRICO: You should pay attention. Juan, the pseudorevolutionary, doesn't know where the money is. We can't afford the PR job, so I suggest we sign with Yuri Brushnik.

ABDUL: But there must be alternatives!

STEPHANIE: Well, I wasn't going to say anything, but now that we're about to go Communist, I guess I should probably tell you that I can get hold of Julio Fernandez.

ENRICO: *What?!*

ABDUL: You *can?!*

STEPHANIE: Yeah. For a price.

ENRICO: Stephanie, what are you talking about?

STEPHANIE: I know where he is. I know he has the money, and I know he has his Versateller card.

KING: Stephanie! How do you know where he is? Did you follow him? Is that why you were late from lunch today?

STEPHANIE: No, I went to Chico's Cantina. You know how slow the service is there.

ENRICO: What's going on, Stephanie?

ABDUL: Tell us.

STEPHANIE: Well, I'm only telling you this because my mother would plotz if I worked for a Communist regime. Julio's been staying at my apartment. He's there now, watching *Gilligan's Island.*

ENRICO: At your *apartment?!*

ABDUL: Watching *Gilligan's Island?!*

KING: But you're not married!

JUAN: You know Julio Fernandez? What's he really like?

TROY: Steph, I gotta tell you, I just knew the minute I saw you that you had yourself a boyfriend. I'm not jealous or anything, that's not the kinda guy I am, but—

ABDUL: Did you say he has his Versateller card with him?

STEPHANIE: Uh-huh.

ENRICO: I want him brought here. This instant.

ABDUL: Absolutely. This instant.

KING: Is he really your boyfriend, Stephanie?

STEPHANIE: Oh—I should've never said anything.

ENRICO: I want him arrested and lynched!

ABDUL: Lynched! After we get his Versateller card, of course.

ENRICO: No, not lynched.

ABDUL: No?

ENRICO: Burned at the stake!

ABDUL: Stoned to death!

ENRICO: Boiled in oil!

STEPHANIE: Oh, enough already! I'll talk to him about forking over the eight million—on one condition.

ENRICO: What?

STEPHANIE: That you don't arrest him.

KING: Oh, that's so romantic!

JUAN: Or me. That you don't arrest me, either.

ENRICO *and* ABDUL: Don't push your luck.

STEPHANIE: So, what do you say?

ENRICO: Well . . .

ABDUL: Your Majesty, what do you think?

KING: I think I'd like to meet him. After all, he *is* Stephanie's boyfriend.

TROY: Yeah, Steph. Invite him over for drinks or something.

ENRICO: This is ridiculous. I want him shot as soon as possible. No ands, ifs, or buts.

STEPHANIE: Well then, I quit.

KING: Stephanie!

STEPHANIE: I thought those revolutionaries were disorganized, but you people are worse than the IRS and AT&T combined! You deserve to be overthrown.

KING *(starting to cry):* You think we're worse than AT&T?

STEPHANIE: And the DMV!

KING: No! Not the Department of Motor Vehicles, too!

ENRICO: Let's have her arrested.

ABDUL: What have I been saying all along? Where did you put the handcuffs?

TROY: Congratulations, Steph. This is a real step forward in your personal growth. At my firm—Barkowitz, Pagnozzi, and LeFlame—we're always looking for a good mail girl or something.

STEPHANIE: Troy, I wouldn't touch Tampa again with a ten-foot dipstick. But thanks anyway.

TROY: Hey! They cleaned up that spill! Just last year, in fact!

ENRICO: Okay, Stephanie. Shut up now. *(Points gun at her.)* Did you find the handcuffs yet, Abdul?

KING: Enrico! Stop that! Guns are not for playing!

ENRICO: Your Majesty, she's a traitor. You know what the punishment is.

KING: Yes, but she can type! We need a typist!

JUAN: I can type.

ABDUL: You're hired.

ENRICO: You never stop interfering, do you, Abdul?

ABDUL: I'm advising.

KING: This is awful! No one else knows how to make Hawaiian Punch! We *can't* shoot Stephanie!

(Enter JULIO *through the window.)*

JULIO *(perched on windowsill):* That's right! Because I'm going to shoot you!

(As he jumps into the room, he trips on JUAN's *sombrero. The gun fires and hits* YURI *in the foot.* YURI, *who has been reading* Southern California Sins, *screams in pain.)*

KING: Yuri!

TROY: Gramps!

STEPHANIE: Julio!

KING: Julio?

ENRICO: There is blood all over the carpet!

ABDUL: Quick, shoot him!

ENRICO: I can't!

ABDUL: Why not?

JULIO: Because *I* stole all your bullets!

KING: Stephanie, call the doctor!

TROY: I was premed. Gramps, are you all right?

YURI: My . . . foot.

KING: He's trying to tell us something.

TROY: He said, "My . . . foot."

ENRICO: Julio shot him in the foot, you morons!

KING: Morons? Enrico! I am the king! You are not the king.

JUAN: Julio, will you sign this? It's for my friend. His name is Juan. Thanks.

(Ambulance arrives, and YURI *is carried out.)*

ENRICO: Look at that. Stephanie, get some towels. What a mess!

STEPHANIE: I quit.

ENRICO: Juan, get some towels.

*(*JUAN *exits.)*
Okay, Julio, put the gun down.

JULIO: No!

STEPHANIE: Just put it down. They're harmless.

JULIO: *Viva la revolución!*

STEPHANIE: Julio.

JULIO: Stephanie! *Viva la revolución!* You have one last request.

ENRICO: Give us your Versateller card.

JULIO: No!

ABDUL: Yes!

JULIO: No!

ENRICO: Do you know what we need it for?

JULIO: *No!*

ENRICO: Tell him, Your Majesty.

KING: Well, Julio, we're planning on getting an amusement park—

TROY: And a pro football team—

ENRICO: And cable TV—

ABDUL: And Club Med—

KING: But we can't afford it, so we'll have to go communist. Do you like communism?

JULIO: No!

STEPHANIE: He's an anarchist.

JULIO: Stephanie!

KING: Phew. So, Julio, won't everybody be happy if we have an amusement park?

JULIO: No!

ABDUL: What about prefab housing?

JULIO: No!

TROY: Not even a new national anthem?

JULIO: N-O *No!* (JULIO *is about to shoot.*)

STEPHANIE: Julio, dear, they're planning on installing a frozen yogurt chain.

JULIO: Really?

ENRICO: Yes, with three flavors daily and ten toppings!

(JULIO *gasps and hands over his Versateller card.*)

KING: I knew you'd come around, Julio.

ABDUL: This is wonderful! Let's celebrate!

(Everyone sings "We all live on the isle of St. Passis.")

KING: Juan, bring some Hawaiian Punch!

STEPHANIE: No, wait, here's the blender. Julio and I stole it last week. Daiquiris, Juan.

(STEPHANIE removes blender from purse and hands it to JUAN. Enter YURI on crutches, wearing sunglasses, shorts, etc.)

JUAN: Excuse me. Do you have an appointment?

YURI: I don't need one.

KING: Yuri Brushnik!

ENRICO: Yuri, how are you?

YURI: I am in much less pain now.

ABDUL: Where did you get those glasses? They look like mine.

YURI: I am proud to announce that I am defecting from the Soviet Union.

KING: That is wonderful!

TROY: Way to go, gramps!

STEPHANIE: What made you decide that?

YURI: When I was shot, my life flashed before my eyes, and I realized that I cannot bear to spend another winter in Leningrad.

ABDUL: I know just how you feel. I couldn't bear to spend another summer in Mecca.

KING: That's when he came to be our adviser. Say, would you like to be our adviser, too, Yuri?

YURI: I'd be honored to.

TROY: Ahem.

KING: And Troy LeFlame! You could be one, too!

ENRICO: Let's not get carried away.

ABDUL: Right. The office is already pretty crowded.

KING: He'd be a splendid adviser, I just know it.

TROY: Aw, gee, thanks. I'd love to be your adviser.

KING: And Stephanie—

STEPHANIE: No way, Your Highness. Julio and I are running off together to Switzerland. Bon voyage!

KING: But first a toast. To St. Passis's latest coup d'etat!

EVERYONE: Cheers! Hear hear! L'chaim! Bottoms up! Olé!

(As everyone is talking, dancing, and drinking, the lights fade, except for a spot on JUAN as he grabs the Versateller card and gun and reclines on the throne, aiming the gun at the KING. Blackout.)

END

CAROLYN JONES

I had lived in San Rafael all my life, in the same bedroom, in fact, until I moved to Santa Cruz to attend the University of California. Now I'm a sophomore at Berkeley.

In high school I was very involved in journalism and liked to envision myself as a female Bob Woodward. I also sold my soul to the Democratic Party shortly before the 1984 New Hampshire Primary. The bitter stupor that followed the election in November, plus a few ulcers from meeting (mostly *not* meeting) newspaper deadlines, led me to abandon all hopes of being a political correspondent for *The Washington Post.* I've written several plays for school, which were produced to encouraging audiences, and have decided that theater is much less disillusioning (and infinitely more fun) than either politics or journalism.

ABOUT THE PLAY

I wrote *Coup d'Etat* for a playwriting contest at school in which first prize was $75. I was obsessively determined—for some last-shot chance at high school immortality—to win. I wrote a play every day for a month and entered them all. Some were better than others, but I thought the sheer volume of my entries would tilt the odds so far in my favor that I couldn't lose. I tied with a freshman.

For years the drama teacher had an outdated Young Playwrights Festival poster hanging in her classroom, and I wondered if the contest still existed. I sent *Coup d'Etat* to the address listed just in case and promptly forgot about it. When I didn't hear for a few months, I figured (a) the contest is indeed defunct, or (b) the play is so bad they didn't want to waste postage on a rejection slip.

When I did hear from them, I was ecstatic, needless to say, and very flattered. But it was also very unreal: there I was, living in Santa Cruz (which is in a perpetual 1969 time warp), trying to believe that these people who kept calling were really from New York (where I had never even been), and were really associated with the Young Playwrights Festival, and were seriously considering a play I had written almost a year ago. In fact, I didn't really believe any of it until I was sitting in the audience watching the New York staged reading in May. And even then I suspected it was a hoax, but a very entertaining one nonetheless.

Living in New York City for six weeks definitely convinced me that the Young Playwrights Festival is indeed a reality, whether I was willing to accept it or not. Every day at rehearsals I saw the play differently. Sometimes I thought it was great; other times I wanted to apologize to every cast member and tech person for putting them through such cruel and unusual punishment. Still, though, I always laughed out loud and enjoyed every performance, with the exception of opening night. If I could do it over again, I'd take more pictures and change Troy LeFlame's last name.

SONATA

BY ELIZABETH HIRSCHHORN
(age fifteen when play was written)
Holyoke, Massachusetts

NOTE:
For the purpose of publication in this collection, certain words
have been changed by the playwright and some profanity has
been deleted from the working script of the play as performed at
Playwrights Horizons, New York City, April 7 through April 28,
1985.

CHARACTERS

LITTLE BOY
LITTLE GIRL
JOSEPH WALLACE
JUDY AMORY
CLARK AMORY
LISA AMORY
MAN'S VOICE

This play is dedicated to my father, for "tempering me in the fires of adversity," and to my mother, for making them even warmer.

NOTE:
When a SOUND is heard, it is projected loudly on speakers throughout the theater so that it invades the thoughts of the audience as well as those of the characters.

PROLOGUE

(The entire stage is dark save for a spotlight downstage right. LITTLE GIRL *and* LITTLE BOY *sit on a large yellow box.)*

LITTLE BOY *(urgency):* Stop flickering, light!

LITTLE GIRL: Now, how did that melody go?

LITTLE BOY: Stop it, stop it now!

LITTLE GIRL: I knew it a moment ago; I truly did.

LITTLE BOY: Stop!

(Lights come on in the area downstage left. The office of Police Detective JOSEPH WALLACE. *Dim, cold lighting suggests the brutal atmosphere of working overtime, late at night. The furniture is simple and strong: a small oak desk littered with papers, a lamp, and coffee cup; an uncomfortable chair.* JOSEPH *stands next to the desk, one foot resting on the chair. He wears gray flannel pants, a white shirt, a bowtie. He is frozen deep in thought. The lighting in the office flickers, first once, then rapidly.)*

JOSEPH: Stop it, light! Stay on, so I can think. Or go out, so I can rest. *(Light is constant; lid is open.)* Now, how did that melody go? *(Hums various melodies; none suit him.)* This morning I stepped into the elevator. "Going down?" "Yes." That song— what *was* it?—Came on. In waves, pounding. "Getting louder?" *(Box is wide open—the office light is bright.)* "Yes." I tried to get out at each level. (LITTLE GIRL *opens the box, which has shut halfway.)*

LITTLE GIRL: Locked in?

(LITTLE BOY shuts it halfway.)

LITTLE BOY: No!

(LITTLE GIRL *opens it again.*)

LITTLE GIRL: Yes!

JOSEPH: And if it weren't in the elevator, it would be somewhere else. In the subway I hear it . . . in the shower . . . in my sleep.

(LITTLE BOY *and* LITTLE GIRL *wave their arms as if conducting. Music comes up. Spot on* BOY *and* GIRL *out.*)

JOSEPH: I have all the evidence. Documents, cassettes, witnesses . . . memory . . . music. I have not been able to accept any more assignments. It has been days, weeks, months. Because there's something about this case that I just can't . . . . I am—I was—a police detective. The family is the Amory family.

(*Spotlight downstage, illuminating, from right to left,* CLARK, LISA, *and* JUDY, *frozen.* JUDY *takes two steps forward, then freezes.*)

JOSEPH: Judith Amory. Age, thirty-two. Hair, red. Eyes, blue. Gray in the rain. Small birthmark under left arm. Occupation, pianist.

MAN'S VOICE: Excuse me, Mr. Wallace. That's housewife, not pianist. We have her listed here as having given up piano.

JOSEPH: Pianist!

MAN'S VOICE (*cold*): As you like, Mr. Wallace.

(SOUND: *click of camera shutter.*)

MAN'S VOICE: Profile please, Mrs. Amory. (JUDY *turns right.*)

(SOUND: *camera click.* JUDY *steps back.* CLARK *steps forward.*)

JOSEPH: Clark Amory. Age, thirty-four. Hair, brown. Eyes, hazel. No distinguishing scars or marks. Occupation, breaker.

MAN'S VOICE: Pardon me, Mr. Wallace, I believe you misread the document. That's *broker*.

JOSEPH: Stockbroker.

(SOUND: camera click.)

MAN'S VOICE: Profile please, Mr. Amory. *(CLARK turns left.)* Turn right, Mr. Amory.

(CLARK turns right. SOUND: camera clicks. CLARK steps back; LISA skips forward, energetic and fidgeting. CLARK and JUDY remain frozen.)

JOSEPH: Lisa Amory. Parents, living.

LISA: Mommy, I don't want to get my picture taken.

JOSEPH: Age, nine and one quarter.

LISA: Can we go now, Daddy? C'mon, please?

JOSEPH: Hair, light brown. Eyes, blue.

LISA: Can we stop at McDonald's after?

JOSEPH: Small scar on sole of right foot.

MAN'S VOICE: Profile please, Lisa.

LISA: What's a profile?

(Spotlight on AMORYS *blacks out.)*

JOSEPH: The Amorys. One twenty-four Cherrywood Avenue, Cedarville. 8:09 A.M.

(Lights on JOSEPH's *office black out, leaving stage dark.)*

SCENE ONE

(The set is an upper-middle-class household, consisting of a living room on the right side of the stage and adjoining kitchen on the left. The living room is pretty, neat, and common. There is a large easy chair in the center of the room, a little to the right. Left of it, in a row, are a stand with The Wall Street Journal *and a telephone on it, and a small camel-back couch. A coffee table is in front of the couch, with a silver bowl of candy on a doily. A television and dry mop are off to the side; a piano is upstage.* LISA *sits at the piano, picking out the melody line of* The Moonlight Sonata *with her right hand. The kitchen is sunny and functional. In the center is a round table with three chairs in a U behind it, and there is a line of appliances upstage.* CLARK's *place is set, right, with coffee.* JUDY's *place is set, left, with yogurt and tea; she is bustling around upstage.* LISA's *place is in the middle, set with Lucky Charms and orange juice.)*

*(*SOUND: *the sizzle of sausage being fried. Lighting brightens.* SOUND *continues)*

JUDY *(hair brushed neatly, wearing crisp pink bathrobe):* I'm not going to call you again, Lisa. Your sausages are almost ready.

LISA: I'm not in the mood for sausages, Mom. *(Continues on piano.)*

(Sizzling SOUND *stops.* JUDY *plops three sausages onto* LISA's *plate from a frying pan.)*

JUDY: You need your protein, dear. Come eat.

LISA: I'm stuffed! Do you want me to barf Lucky Charms all over the school bus?

JUDY: I don't like that language, sweetie.

LISA *(entering kitchen):* What, *barf?*

JUDY: Try to eat one sausage.

LISA: Why don't you send them to some starving child in Cambodia or something?

(CLARK enters right, crosses to kitchen with briefcase and the New York Times. *He wears a conservative suit.)*

JUDY: Fine. You fly yourself over to Cambodia, and I'll send them to you Federal Express.

CLARK *(entering kitchen, concerned):* What's going on in Cambodia *now? (Not overly serious.)* That country is a source of continuous consternation. Someone really ought to blow it off the map.

JUDY *(laughs):* Clark! Moderation.

CLARK: It would put an end to starving refugees—

LISA: I don't have to eat if I don't want to, do I, Daddy?

CLARK *(sits, opens* New York Times): What? Of course not, munchkin.

LISA *(to* JUDY): See?

JUDY *(annoyed):* How can I keep discipline around here if you give in to Lisa every time I tell her to do something?

CLARK: She shouldn't have to eat if she isn't hungry.

JUDY: Since when are you the nutrition expert in the family?

CLARK: Eat your food, Lisa.

LISA: But you *said* . . .

CLARK: Listen to Mommy.

JUDY (contentedly): One bite, dear. (LISA takes the tiniest bite she can.)

LISA: The softball team needs another mother to drive to the game tomorrow, Mom.

JUDY: I'd volunteer, dear, but tomorrow's not a good day for me. I have a hairdresser appointment, and it's marketing and vacuuming day. You should have let me know sooner.

LISA (meekly): I already said you would.

JUDY: Lisa Lynn! How could you—

LISA: I know I should have asked first, Mommy, but I forgot, and, well, none of the other mothers could do it, and I said you were the best and you always have time for me, and everyone's counting on you, and look—I'm eating a sausage. (She stuffs a large bite into her mouth.)

JUDY (sighs): What time do you need me?

LISA: One thirty. Thanks, Mom.

CLARK (chuckles): I'm glad to see we're not giving in on disciplinary matters.

LISA: Will you come to my game, Daddy?

CLARK: I'd love to, but you know I have to work.

LISA (whining): But you said you'd come to my next game!

CLARK: And I'd like to very much, but I have to work. If I didn't work, who would pay for your uniform?

LISA (carefully): Mom's coming.

CLARK: Mom doesn't work during the day—at an office. I'll come to your next game, I promise.

LISA: You promised last time. Connie's daddy was there. Connie's daddy is always there.

CLARK: Connie's daddy is a bank president. He doesn't have to work.

JUDY *(quickly):* Daddy will come to your tournament Saturday.

CLARK: That's right. Wouldn't miss it.

LISA: Okay—I guess.

JUDY: Now, go! You'll miss your bus.

LISA: I'm going. Bye, Mom. *(She picks up lunch bag and jacket, avoids CLARK.)*

CLARK: Wait a minute. Aren't you forgetting something?

LISA *(haughtily):* I don't think you deserve a kiss today, Daddy.

CLARK: Please?

LISA: Oh, all right. *(Sitting on CLARK's knee, she gives him a kiss on the cheek.)*

JUDY *(impatiently):* The bus won't wait.

LISA: I'm going! *(Moves toward door, left.)*

JUDY: Love you, dear. Put that jacket on.

LISA *(exits, carrying jacket):* It's hot out.

(Silence. She clears the table and he reads The New York Times.*)*

JUDY: Listen, you'll have to heat up your own dinner Wednesday night. *(Proud.)* I have a potluck supper.

CLARK: You know I hate that, honey.

JUDY: I know. I'm sorry. But I have to go. The new head of the PTA is going to speak. Mary O'Neill. I hear she's very well educated. And intelligent. She went to Smith College. Anyway, I have to go. I'll make a chicken today. How about chicken à l'orange?

CLARK: Fine, fine. *(Muttering.)* What do you do at all these potluck suppers? Don't you get sick of macaroni salads?

JUDY: I'll have you know my macaroni salads are famous, Clark. Everyone loves them. And this is a social event. I see all the girls. We learn a lot from the speakers, too. Last month the guest speaker was a woman who spent six years sewing shirts for pregnant women in Lebanon.

CLARK *(glancing at watch):* Well, looks like I'm almost late. I have a meeting at nine.

(He kisses her quickly and exits left with briefcase. JUDY *shuffles into the living room and begins to clean, picking up* LISA's *clothes, books, toys. She flips on the TV.* SOUND: *female voice counting out aerobic exercises to music.* JUDY *attempts to follow along and has increasing difficulty as the workout becomes faster. Out of breath and annoyed, she gives up, turns off the TV, and resumes cleaning. When she reaches the piano, she runs her fingers over the polished keys and quickly looks around before sitting eagerly to play. She begins* The Moonlight Sonata, *playing with deep expression until she hits incorrect keys. She begins the bar again and ends again in error. Frustrated, she bangs her hands on the keys and then gazes at her fingers, holding them up to the light.)*

SCENE TWO

(Lights brighten on JOSEPH *in his office.)*

MAN'S VOICE: Another missing kid case, Wallace.

JOSEPH: Another missing child case. Thursday morning. Nine thirty-seven A.M.

MAN'S VOICE: The little girl in question never made it to the school bus yesterday. Disappeared. Parents'll be in at ten. Better give 'em the special treatment.

JOSEPH: I prepared the special treatment. *(He sets things up as he speaks.)* Coffee, to calm the worried couple's nerves. Tissues, for the grieving mother. Forms to fill out: regulation. Pencils, because they always forget writing implements in their rush.

*(*JUDY *and* CLARK *enter, right.)*

CLARK: Yes, I'm sure, honey. He's supposed to be very good. He was written up in the *Tribune* about that Wescott case.

JUDY: Well, what about that little boy two summers ago that they never found. Wasn't that Mr. Wallace?

JOSEPH *(at door of office, interrupting):* You must be the Amorys. Come in. *(He sets up two stools for them.)* Sit down. Please make yourselves comfortable.

*(*CLARK *and* JUDY *sit, silent.* JOSEPH *glances at the audience.)* Coffee?

CLARK: No. No, thank you.

JUDY: We had some before we came.

JOSEPH *(surprised at their refusal):* Well then, we ought to get on with things. Do you have a picture of Lisa?

JUDY: Of course. *(She pulls a photo from her purse.)* Here. (JOSEPH *takes it.)* That's my little girl. It's not a good picture. Doesn't show her eyes. My eyes.

JOSEPH: This one will do nicely, Mrs. Amory. *(Jots down notes on a pad.)* Can you tell me what Lisa was last seen wearing?

JUDY: She was wearing a bluish lavender sweater, acrylic, with pink hearts and white dogs—Scottish terriers—in a Fair Isle pattern across the yoke; and pink corduroy pants, wide wale, and a tannish jacket with red plaid—

CLARK: No, honey, she wasn't wearing a jacket.

JUDY: Yes, she was! I laid it out for her myself with her lunch and books. A tannish color canvas, with red plaid—

CLARK: I remember very clearly. You told her to put the jacket on and she said, "It's hot."

JUDY: There, you see? Whether she was wearing it or not, she did have it with her.

CLARK: But Mr. Wallace asked us what she was *last seen wearing.*

JOSEPH: Excuse me.

JUDY: Listen to us. You must think we're terrible.

JOSEPH: Quite the contrary, Mrs. Amory. I'll give you some forms to fill out now.

(He holds out a set of papers, and CLARK *takes them. As he produces the pens he got out earlier,* JUDY *extracts two pencils from her purse and hands one to* CLARK.)

JUDY: We expected there would be forms.

JOSEPH *(rising, awkward):* Did Lisa have any reason to run away from home? Did she show any signs of unhappiness . . . withdrawal . . . problems at school?

JUDY: Absolutely not. My daughter is a very happy, well-adjusted girl. She has friends, lots of them, just like I did when I was a girl. Isn't that right, Clark?

CLARK: Certainly. Lisa's doing fine at school. Brings home A's and B's, always has a good attitude report.

JOSEPH: Yes, I'm sure she's a bright young lady. Has Lisa ever been abused?

CLARK: No.

JUDY: Of course not!

JOSEPH: And would you say she feels your love at home?

JUDY: Are you implying that we're not good parents?

JOSEPH: It's a routine question, Mrs. Amory. You're going to have to bear with me on these. Nine out of ten disappearances today are runaways.

JUDY: My daughter is not a runaway! She has no reason; why, she has a softball game tomorrow! How could she run away? She has everything at home. Good food, a nice school, love—

CLARK: Lisa is very, uh, content at home. I give her a kiss goodbye when she leaves for school each morning, the little munchkin. We make peanut butter and banana sandwiches at night, "heavy on the p.b., hold the jelly," when she doesn't want to go to bed. And every once in a while, when she's asleep, I come up and tuck her in. I listen to the even, soft breathing, brush the hair off her smooth little forehead. You know, sometimes I think I love her the most when she's asleep. Oh, I don't mean I don't love her when she's awake, but when those soft eyelashes flutter—

JOSEPH: Kiss each morning . . . hold the jelly . . . love her most . . . tuck her in . . . flutter . . . his little girl.

Interlude One

(Spotlight downstage right on LITTLE BOY *and* LITTLE GIRL, *bouncing rubber ball back and forth.)*

LITTLE BOY: God, they're weird.

LITTLE GIRL: Who?

LITTLE BOY: You know, the Grieving Parents.

LITTLE GIRL: It's not proper to pass judgments on others when you really don't know. That's what Mummy says.

LITTLE BOY: Oh, screw Mummy!

LITTLE GIRL *(shocked. Grabs ball.):* I'm not going to play with you anymore if you're going to be like that.

LITTLE BOY: Don't, then!

LITTLE GIRL: I rather pity them. *(Trying to make up.)* Don't you?

LITTLE BOY: I thought we're not playing together anymore.

(Spotlight blacks out.)

SCENE THREE

(Lights brighten in the living room. It is late evening. JUDY sits on the camel-backed couch, reading Self *magazine and clutching her handkerchief. CLARK is in his chair, reading* Business Week. *JUDY sniffs periodically, flipping her pages rapidly. CLARK stares blankly at his magazine.)*

JUDY: It's so quiet.

CLARK: No TV.

JUDY: No math homework.

CLARK: No after-dinner snacks.

(JUDY begins to cry.)

CLARK: Don't start again. Don't start crying again.

JUDY: It's not fair! We don't deserve this.

CLARK: Things like this just happen, I guess. Freak things. Unexpected.

JUDY: Why?

CLARK: Anything can happen. Like when Marion left Harry for that Italian poet. They were a perfect couple. And then Marion just left one day. No one deserved that.

JUDY *(to herself, not responding to* CLARK*)*: Why?

CLARK: Judy.

(No response.)

CLARK: We will get her back.

SCENE FOUR

JOSEPH: I talked to Lisa's friends. Cute little girls. They said when Lisa didn't show up at the bus stop, they figured she was sick. Sweet little things. One of them was crying. She grabbed my coat and . . . I hugged her. I hugged her.

Interlude Two

(Spotlight on LITTLE GIRL *and* LITTLE BOY, *downstage right.* LITTLE GIRL *is sitting, doing embroidery on a ring.* LITTLE BOY *is playing cops and robbers by himself.)*

LITTLE BOY: So, where's Lisa?

LITTLE GIRL: I don't know.

LITTLE BOY: Do so!

LITTLE GIRL: Do not!

LITTLE BOY: Do so!

LITTLE GIRL: Do not!

LITTLE BOY *(pointing out into audience):* She's up in that tree.

LITTLE GIRL: So get her down.

LITTLE BOY: I can't reach her.

LITTLE GIRL *(looking into audience):* She's not even there!

LITTLE BOY: I never said she was.

SCENE FIVE

(It is morning, days later. CLARK and JUDY are seated at the kitchen table eating breakfast. Newspapers are spread out on the table, and they are both reading. LISA's place is set with the box of Lucky Charms. JUDY's bathrobe is rumpled, and her hair mussed. CLARK is wearing his usual pressed suit but has gray circles under his eyes.)

JUDY: Just think. Today could be the day when someone sits down to breakfast, sees Lisa's picture in the *Tribune,* and says, "Hey! I just saw that little girl." Then they'll call, and we'll get her back.

CLARK: You know what Joseph said about waiting. It is long, and it is painful.

JUDY: I think I'll call the newspaper after breakfast and see if any calls have come in. Then I'll call Joseph.

CLARK: Joseph said he'd contact us as soon as anything happens. I don't think we should keep bothering him.

JUDY *(tearful):* Am I really a bother?

CLARK: No, no. But if we leave Joseph alone to think, maybe he'll come up with something.

JUDY: I'm not stopping him from thinking.

CLARK: Fine. Do what you want. Call Joseph.

JUDY: Not if you think I'd be bothering him. That's what you said, isn't it? That I'd be ruining his thinking process? I'll call the *Tribune* and leave it at that.

CLARK: Okay.

JUDY: Or would I be upsetting their workday, too?

CLARK *(exasperated):* Anything you want is good.

JUDY: All right. I'll call after breakfast.

CLARK: Good.

JUDY: Clark?

CLARK: What!

JUDY: Is there anything I can do for you today?

CLARK: What do you mean?

JUDY: Oh, I don't know. Dry cleaning. Mending. I could reorganize your closet.

CLARK: You did all that yesterday.

JUDY: Did I?

CLARK: Why don't you do something for yourself today? There must be a thousand things you've been telling yourself you don't have the time to do. Well, now you have a little free time. I wish I could take the day off to be with you, but I have to work. Come on, what can you indulge in?

JUDY: I don't know.

CLARK: You could go out to lunch with the girls.

JUDY: They can't see me like this!

CLARK: I know, you can play some piano! Surprise me with a song when I come home. I haven't heard you play at all lately.

(Content with his suggestion, he goes back to reading the paper. JUDY looks around the room nervously.)

JUDY: I don't think I'm up to that. There must be some housework I've forgotten.

CLARK: Look. I just saw in the paper. Will you look at this? *(Reads from paper.)* The Cedarville School of Music and Dance needs a part-time teacher for beginning piano students. Why don't you drop over there today?

JUDY: I couldn't handle a job right now! Besides, I told you, I can't play. It—the melody—doesn't come out of me the way it used to.

CLARK *(forcefully):* Come on, Judy! Stop with your excuses! You are a pianist.

JUDY: I thought I'd catch up on some soaps today. I think I'm getting a migraine.

CLARK: Damn it! I am her father! But I go on! Work goes on! And you. You can't watch soap operas all day, day after day! You haven't gotten dressed all week. You are beginning to look terrible. And will you stop eating those chocolates?

JUDY *(throwing down Russell Stover box):* All right! Okay! Just leave me alone. You think life is so easy for me. You and your damn office. Well, you are right. "Mommy *doesn't* work during the day at an office." This family is my work!

CLARK: You work very hard here, I know—

JUDY *(cutting him off):* Damn right I do! I used to practice piano three hours a day. When Lisa was in nursery school and her play group. But I took her out of that play group. We agreed. She's my daughter, I played with her. Brownies, ballet. No more time for my music. Even when she started taking piano lessons, I couldn't get back into it. The day she—two weeks ago, I tried to play *The Moonlight Sonata.* You remember, my first recital piece? I couldn't get through the third bar!

CLARK: You are a successful mother, Judy.

JUDY: I used to warm up with the first movement. Just let my fingers glide over the keys. Ebba used to tell me I have a feel for Beethoven.

CLARK *(guilt heats his face, his hands):* I never knew . . . how you felt. I thought . . .

SCENE SIX

(*Lights on* JOSEPH *in his office. He is exhausted and overworked. His tie is untied, and he is in need of a good shave.*)

JOSEPH: Judy, like most Devastated Mothers, was having trouble adjusting. Clark was playing the strong Grieving Father very well. It was I who needed help. No one had seen Lisa—or no one was telling. The chief was on my back night and day. I had to find the kid.

My next move was wide-scale publicity.

(*Lights on* JOSEPH *fade to a dim spot. He sets up a small television on his desk. Stagehands in gray uniforms wheel a television light or cameras and two stools.* JUDY *and* CLARK *enter from right. A stagehand directs them to the stools, and they sit.*)

MAN'S VOICE: That's right, Amorys. Sit right there. Check spotlights two and four, will you, Charlie?

(*A spotlight blinks, then focuses on the Amorys.*)

MAN'S VOICE: Okay, Amorys. You're on. Four, three, two, one.

(*Sound: News music. Fades.*)

JUDY: We're on? Oh! (*She pats hair.*)

CLARK (*To the audience: Loud, clear*): Our daughter, Lisa Lynn Amory, disappeared from our street on her way to the school bus April second. The police believe she was kidnapped.

JUDY: I watched her run out the door that morning, as cheerful as a little girl can be, to catch up with her friends at the bus stop. How was I to know she would never come home? That my baby would be taken from me? What kind of world do we live in?

CLARK: Lisa loves to play softball and to go out with her Girl Scout troop. She's a spirited little thing.

JUDY: So why us? Why? Our lives are very . . . empty without Lisa.

CLARK: We are asking you to help us. You out there, who have your own little girl or boy safe at home.

MAN'S VOICE: In a moment, you will see Lisa's picture on your television screen.

JUDY: We want our baby back! Please!

MAN'S VOICE: If you have seen Lisa, kindly call toll-free: one eight hundred . . .

(Lights brighten on JOSEPH. *He shuts off the television, which turns off the* MAN'S VOICE *and the spotlight off* JUDY *and* CLARK.*)*

JOSEPH: A pretty good presentation, don't you think? Poignant, touching. Gave thousands a good cry. All kinds of people called in. Not with leads or clues, but with sympathy. There were housewives who wanted to start a "Help Lisa" fund. Families calling to donate kittens, puppies. But no clues. *(Pause.)* It was two weeks before I saw the Amorys again.

(A dim light has appeared in the Amory household as JOSEPH *speaks.* JUDY *and* CLARK *enter downstage right. They cross to center, walk upstage to the living room, sit on the couch, and freeze.)*

They kind of drifted away from me, the Amorys. Judy got herself a part-time job. Clark got his promotion.

(Stagehand brings in a flower arrangement from upstage right, sets it on the piano, and exits. Another stagehand crosses in from downstage left in front of JOSEPH's *office, carrying a bottle of liquor. He sets it on the newspaper stands and exits right.)*

They still called me . . . every other night or so.

(Stagehand enters through kitchen, places flower arrangement on floor, and exits right.)
But I was afraid they were losing faith in me, or just losing faith.

(Stagehand enters right, sets liquor tray on television set, and exits.)

JOSEPH: They should have known I would never give up! I would not lose Lisa, like the others! *(Pause.)* I was glad to see them keeping busy, of course. *(As if trying to convince himself.)* Of course.

(Lights black out.)

SCENE SEVEN

(Early evening in the Amory household. CLARK *and* JUDY *are dressing up.)*

JUDY *(crossing from right to left to pick up pocketbook and exit again):* It certainly was nice of the mayor to invite us over for tea, honey.

CLARK *(entering right, in a well-tailored blazer, tying tie):* And remember—Bill and Susan Harmon are taking us out on their yacht next Sunday. Bill says once we get a taste of that salt spray, we'll run right out and buy our own schooner. *(Exits right.)*

JUDY: Do you think there'll be more photographers there, Clark?

(Enters living room, primping. Wears pretty spring dress, young, fresh hairstyle, and makeup. She is radiant.)

CLARK: *(off right)* And Bill says Rockman says I really deserved the promotion—they're all glad I got it over Martin. "The man on the job," he called me, "Inspiration, youthful vigor, perseverance." *(Enters living room.)*

JUDY *(indicating her appearance):* Well?

CLARK: Stunning!

JUDY: You like it? I got it at Magrams yesterday—on sale. If you don't—

CLARK: I like you. *(Appropriate action—perhaps grabs her.)*

JUDY: Clark . . . you'll mess up my hair. What if the press is at the mayor's? Clark!

CLARK: What?

JUDY: You can't wear that tie. You really can't. *(Exits to bedroom.)*

CLARK: Hey, honey? You know, I was thinking. In return for all these invitations we've been getting, we ought to have a cocktail party or something.

(JUDY returns and replaces his tie with a new one during the following dialogue.)

JUDY: A cocktail party! I've always wanted to have a real cocktail party. I found some fantastic recipes for pâté and hors d'oeuvres in this month's *Gourmet*. And Marona, she's the—

CLARK *and* JUDY: Owner of the School of Music—

JUDY: —has cocktail parties all the time, so I've heard.

CLARK: How are you doing at the school now, anyway?

JUDY: Oh, I love it! I really do. Remember I told you about Timothy? He's coming along so well. Even after just two lessons. He can almost play his C scale with both hands at once. I feel like I'm helping him so much.

CLARK: You ought to ask Marona to help you analyze your playing.

JUDY: I'm going to. Maybe she'll tell me . . . I still have my flair for concertos.

(Lights out.)

Interlude Three

(Spotlight downstage right on LITTLE BOY *and* LITTLE GIRL. LIT-
TLE GIRL *is drawing on the floor with chalk.* LITTLE BOY *is playing Indian by himself.)*

LITTLE GIRL: Can I join in?

LITTLE BOY: No! *(He unties the bow in her hair mischievously
and laughs hysterically.)*

LITTLE GIRL: Why did you do that? Mummy will be angry. (LIT-
TLE BOY *resumes Indian play.* LITTLE GIRL *stands up, pointedly,
and draws chalk line across stage between them.* LITTLE BOY
watches, confused and fascinated.)

LITTLE BOY *(wide-eyed):* What's that for?

LITTLE GIRL: You may not cross this line. You may not speak to
me; you may not play with me; you may not watch *them* with
me.

(They face each other on either side of the line, fists clenched.)

LITTLE BOY: And if I step over the line? *(He crosses it, stands
next to her.)*

LITTLE GIRL: Then *I* will step over the line. *(She moves to the
other side.)*

(He chases her in circles, both shrieking. Spotlight blacks out.)

SCENE EIGHT

(Lights flash on in JOSEPH's *office.* JOSEPH, *unshaven and disheveled, has dozed off at his desk. Lights flicker. He wakes up, grunting, and climbs on desk.)*

JOSEPH: I will not hit you, light. I will count to three, and if you have not begun to behave, I will smash you. One . . . Two . . . *(Light is constant.)*

(In this scene MAN'S VOICE *is* JOSEPH'S CHIEF.)

CHIEF: Wallace!

JOSEPH *(stepping down hurriedly)*: Chief! Didn't hear you come in. Just changing a light bulb. *(Glances intermittently at doorway.)*

CHIEF *(amused)*: Of course you are. A delicate procedure. *(Cold.)* Have you gone through today's mail yet?

JOSEPH: No, chief. *(Shuffles stack of letters on desk nervously.)*

CHIEF: You know what's there, Wallace. And you're afraid of it! You are terrified because the public wants that Amory girl found, and you are failing. Twenty-six years on the police force, Wallace, and how many missing children cases have you left in the "unresolved" drawer? How many times have you flubbed up? How many? You've got to try harder! And read the letters. Go ahead. How does that one on the top of the stack begin? Come on. Let's hear it. "I am ashamed . . ."

JOSEPH: ". . . for my country that mothers' babies are allowed to be plucked off the street like grapes"—like grapes?—"and never returned home."

CHIEF: And the next one?

JOSEPH: Read it! "I am disappointed at the . . . at the . . ."

JOSEPH *and* CHIEF: *Incompetence.*

JOSEPH *(reading):* ". . . of your so-called staff." Okay. I see. It stings.

CHIEF: And the next?

JOSEPH: Must we?

CHIEF: "My heart . . ."

JOSEPH: We both know what it says!

CHIEF: "My heart . . ."

JOSEPH: Please!

CHIEF: "My heart . . ."

JOSEPH: All right. You've made your point.

CHIEF: "My heart . . . goes out to the . . ."

CHIEF *and* JOSEPH: ". . . young innocent . . ."

JOSEPH: ". . . who no one can help."

JOSEPH: But I will. I must!

CHIEF: Find her.

(Sound: Door slamming.)

Interlude Four

(Brief. Spot downstage right. LITTLE BOY *is still on one side of the line, now sprawled out on the floor, crying his heart out.* LITTLE GIRL *is on the other side, sitting with her knees pressed to her chin, swaying back and forth, humming* The Moonlight Sonata.*)*

SCENE NINE

(*Lights switch to living room.* JUDY *is in* CLARK's *chair reading* The Wall Street Journal. CLARK *is in the kitchen cooking.*)

JUDY: Mmmmm. A twenty-two-point climb in three days. (*Shouts to* CLARK.) Hey, did you read this, honey? Restaurants and transports are at rock bottom, but fossil fuels are way up. What do you say, a hundred Exxon and five or so Shared Medical Systems?

(CLARK *has a towel draped over his shoulder. He is working on a cake at the kitchen table.*)

CLARK: All right, honey. My ice cream pineapple upside-down cake is going to be the highlight of the meal. A pinch of cinnamon, a touch of orange peel—oh, so finely grated—a dollop of ginger, and (*puts it in the refrigerator*) another great male chef.

(*Sound: Doorbell.*)

JUDY: That must be Joseph. Would you let him in? I just want to go freshen up.

(JUDY *exits right.* CLARK *opens the kitchen door.* JOSEPH *enters, and* CLARK *shakes his hand heartily.* JOSEPH *has combed his hair and put on his bowtie but looks gray and weary.*)

CLARK: Joseph! Nice to see you again. It's been a few days since—

JOSEPH: Two weeks. Hello, Mr. Amory.

CLARK: Clark, Clark. Never could understand why you call me Mister. Come in, come in. Judy's upstairs changing into something ravishing, and dinner is all prepared.

JOSEPH: I really can't stay for dinner. I tried to convey that to Mrs. Amory on the phone.

CLARK: I'll fix you a drink. What'll you have—Scotch, a martini?

JOSEPH: I have finishing up to do at the office.

CLARK: She and the housekeeper have made a fantastic roast. They've been bustling around for hours. You know how women are.

(CLARK *hands* JOSEPH *a drink.*)

JOSEPH: I really shouldn't. *(Takes drink.)* Now. *(Moves toward couch.)*

CLARK: Take the big chair.

JOSEPH: It's all right. That's your chair. Now. *(Sits on the couch. JUDY enters. JOSEPH stands, bumping coffee table.)* Hello.

JUDY: No, no. Don't stand.

JOSEPH: Hello, Mrs. Amory. You're looking well.

JUDY: Why, thank you, Joseph. I've been getting a lot of beauty rest lately. How did you like that last TV appearance? *The Thirty Minutes with Tom Simmons Show?*

JOSEPH: It was very . . . touching, Mrs. Amory.

JUDY: Oh, you mean when I stood up and shouted, "We live in a corrupt world!" don't you? I don't know what came over me— the heat of the moment, I guess.

(JOSEPH *drinks the entire martini in one defeated gulp.* CLARK *refills his glass.*)

CLARK: Quite a change from that first TV spot, isn't it? Got rid of that stage fright. Took charge of the situation, she did.

JOSEPH (hiccups, relaxed.): I've always had stage fright. Even when I was a kid. I remember the first time—the Christmas pageant. You know the sort; fifth-grade class, Miss Sullivan running the show.

JUDY: Yes. I used to have stage fright, too. At each piano recital, I remember shaking so hard—

JOSEPH: A little girl in my class wrote the play. The whole class worked on this play for three weeks straight. (JUDY and CLARK exchange glances; JOSEPH is absorbed in his tale.) I was a scrawny kid, so I got the part of some elf. (He finishes off his second drink.)

CLARK (politely): Hmph! An elf!

JUDY: Fancy that!

JOSEPH (marveling): An elf!

CLARK: Have an hors d'oeuvre.

JOSEPH: So anyway, there I was on pageant night, waiting to recite my line, my one short line.

(CLARK fidgets at the liquor tray. JUDY sits on the arm of the chair, picking at a pulled thread.)

JOSEPH: I was scanning the audience as I stood there. A child in the audience caught my eye. I watched the kid, maybe four or five years old. He was pulling on his mother's sleeve.

(JUDY moves around the room, touching cards, gifts.)

But what got me was, she hit him. Smacked him! Hard! On the top of the head. I was shocked.

(JUDY moves to the piano. CLARK does not move.)

As I stood there, in my pointed cardboard ears and green bloomers, watching the kid sob, I noticed silence on the stage. In the middle of the play. Silence. *(Silence.)* And then I knew they were all waiting for me . . . to say my line. And the problem was, I couldn't remember my line. A little girl up onstage started crying, then, because I had ruined the play. Her play.

(Pause.)

CLARK: Imagine that. Do you remember the line now?

JOSEPH: What? Oh . . . uh . . . no.

JUDY: And now, gentlemen, Ms. Judith Amory will perform for you a timeless classic. (JUDY *sits at the piano, begins to play a section of* The Moonlight Sonata.*)*

JOSEPH: I remember the look on the kid's face—distraction. I remember vowing never to let myself get distracted from delivering my line again.

CLARK: Interesting story, Joseph. I never went for the theater much as a kid, though. Can I fill your glass, Joseph?

JOSEPH: I've had quite enough, thank you. I've decided you should offer a reward.

CLARK: What?

JOSEPH: For Lisa's safe return. You'd be surprised how money talks.

CLARK: You know Judy and I are eager to help in any way we can.

JOSEPH: What I'm driving at is those personal donations people are sending. A few are coming to the station, and we put them ight into the budget. But I believe many are coming to you at ome.

CLARK: Yes, as a matter of fact.

JOSEPH: How much do you have?

CLARK (*flustered, attempting a smile*): Well, I don't know, exactly.

JOSEPH (*forcefully*): Surely you must have some idea, some record. You are a businessman, Mr. Amory. While the money is legally yours to use as you please, the police force likes to record the figures. The chief keeps very organized accounts, Mr. Amory. (*Song is at climax.*)

CLARK (*uncomfortable*): Actually, Joe, I've invested a couple of the checks. International Paper and Revlon are on an uprise. I thought I'd make a little extra, so we'd have more to spend on Lisa when we get her back. College is expensive, you know.

JOSEPH (*coldly*): Reward money might very well help.

CLARK (*embarrassed*): I'll be glad to write you a check anytime. Just name your amount.

JUDY, *having finished her song, approaches the men from upstage. Both men are startled by her sudden presence.*)

JOSEPH (to JUDY): You have quite a talent.

JUDY: Why, thank you. And what have you boys been chatting about?

CLARK: Joseph thinks we should offer a reward.

JUDY: That's an idea!

JOSEPH: We've had mixed results with rewards in the past, Mrs. Amory. Most often they're useless.

JUDY: You know best, Joseph.

CLARK: Shouldn't you be checking the roast?

JUDY: Oh! I almost forgot!

JOSEPH *(rising):* I must be going. I told you I couldn't stay for dinner.

JUDY: But I thought—

JOSEPH: I'll be getting in touch with you.

CLARK: Thanks for stopping by, Joseph. And we'll talk later about a reward. You—you're the boss. *(JOSEPH exits through the kitchen.)*

JUDY: What about my roast? I had everything set for three.

CLARK *(sexy, suave):* How about a romantic candlelight dinner for two instead? You know what they say about crowds.

JUDY: Candlelight?

CLARK *(savage):* Or total darkness.

JUDY *(surprised):* Well, I guess so.

(JUDY exits right. CLARK sets coffee table with wine, candles, and a single rose he takes from a flower arrangement. Whistling The Moonlight Sonata, *he undoes his tie and unbuttons his top shirt buttons. As he dims a small table lamp, the entire set becomes romantically dark. He lights the candles. JUDY enters right, wearing a kimono. CLARK sweeps her into a long kiss.)*

CLARK: You smell fantastic.

JUDY: So—so do you.

CLARK: What perfume are you wearing? Savage Musk? Today's Woman? Ninja?

JUDY *(blushing):* No. First Time.

CLARK: May I propose a toast, then, to the famous pianist, who shall someday sing her lovely fingertips across only the finest pianos of the world. *(They drink.)*

JUDY: And I would like to propose a toast to my illustrious Wall Street tycoon. *(They drink.)*

CLARK *(playfully):* Okay, Judy, sit down.

JUDY: What?

CLARK: Shut your eyes.

JUDY: A surprise!

CLARK: I was going to save this for our anniversary. Maybe I shouldn't tell you.

JUDY: No, tell me, tell me!

CLARK: Well . . . okay. Shut your eyes. *(He shuts them with his fingertips.)*

JUDY: I'm ready.

(CLARK produces a colored pamphlet.)

CLARK: One second, my dear. All right, open! (JUDY *grabs the pamphlet.)* Would you like to join me in an eight-day vacation to Acapulco, Mexico?

JUDY: Oh, Clark!

CLARK (*his voice deepens, as in a commercial*): A cozy four-room seaside apartment. Living room. Kitchen, bedroom, and sun porch equipped with jacuzzi, the sun, me.

JUDY: I love you, I really do. Just like our honeymoon.

(*They snuggle together on the couch. Kiss.* CLARK *blows out candles; stage is black.*)

Interlude Five

(*Spotlight on* LITTLE BOY *and* LITTLE GIRL *downstage right. They are seated facing one another, playing a rhythm game: knees, clap, snap, snap. Knees, clap, snap, snap. Beat is steady, like a heartbeat. They speak on beats.*)

LITTLE GIRL: Beat, beat, beat, beat.

LITTLE BOY: Beat, beat, beat, beat.

LITTLE GIRL: Beat, beat, Lee, Lee.

LITTLE BOY: Beat, beat, Lee-sa

LITTLE GIRL (*knees, clap*): Lis-sa

LITTLE BOY (*knees, clap*): Lisa is . . .

LITTLE GIRL (*knees*): Lisa is . . . (*About to snap last beat and speak.*)

(*Blackout.*)

SCENE TEN

(JOSEPH *is pacing excitedly up and down his office, carrying the* *telephone. He interrupts* LITTLE BOY *and* LITTLE GIRL. *Papers* *and coffee mugs are strewn all over the room.*)

JOSEPH *(shouting):* A clue, a clue, a clue! And where are you, Amorys? Why don't you answer the phone?

SCENE ELEVEN

(Lights shine brightly along front edge of stage. SOUND: intermittent birds chirping; other outdoor spring sounds. Stagehand has placed park bench downstage right. JUDY and CLARK enter downstage left. They walk leisurely around JOSEPH's office to the front edge of the stage and continue right, holding hands.)

JUDY: Did I tell you I got a letter from Marion today? She's living in Manhattan now.

CLARK: With that greasy little Italian character?

JUDY: Frederico is a very nice man. He's been good for Marion. She's gotten back into her sculpting. He does all the cooking and housework.

CLARK: But what about poor Harry? All alone.

JUDY: Come on now. Harry is a drunk and a flirt. Marion deserves better. God only knows why she didn't leave sooner.

CLARK: Harry's a great guy! The greatest cross he ever had to bear was being the victim of PTA meeting gossip.

JUDY: Oh, no!

CLARK: What?

JUDY: There's a potluck supper tonight. I completely forgot!

(They have come to the park bench, and they sit.)

CLARK: I suppose I could heat up some avocado chicken or something.

JUDY: No. I won't go. I won't leave you home alone. Besides, I was supposed to bring macaroni salad, and I don't even have any of the ingredients.

CLARK: Well, we could pick some of them up at the corner grocery.

JUDY: No. Just forget it. I won't go.

CLARK: This is a first! You've never missed a potluck supper. *(Pronounces "potluck supper" with respect, jokingly.)* Never. I thought they all depended on your macaroni salads.

JUDY: I am not going. I hate potluck suppers.

CLARK: Why in the world . . . ?

JUDY: Because they'd have talked about me if I didn't go all these years. They used to be kind of fun. A real get-together for the girls. To get out of the house. But then they got bad. Who could look the youngest? Everyone gossiping about who's on the latest fad diet.

CLARK: Or who hides the German chocolate cake in the laundry hamper.

JUDY: Who has a summerhouse? Who went to Australia last winter?

CLARK: Whose husband is playing around?

JUDY: Clark! No. *(Grins.)* I wish they had.

CLARK: I would have gone.

JUDY: Maybe it wouldn't have all been so boring. *(Pause.)* I just don't need any of that now.

CLARK: Well, well, well.

JUDY *(changing the subject, hurriedly):* Hey, how long has it been since we've taken a walk together on a Thursday afternoon?

CLARK: I don't know. Ages. We used to go to softball . . . games.

JUDY: Smell the lilacs, Clark.

CLARK: Spring. Let's pick some wild flowers.

JUDY: We have a house full of flowers.

CLARK: Those aren't real flowers.

JUDY: It's lovely of people to send them to us. Those that don't know us bearing gifts. Our friends—our secret friends.

CLARK: Our friends?

JUDY *(loudly):* I'm even getting gifts at the school.

CLARK: Gifts?

JUDY: Yes, gifts!

CLARK: Can't you see what they're doing to us? These gifts, these "friends"? Constant reminders of our loss—that's what they are. Do they think we need reminding? To be told she's gone? Do they think we want to grieve every day, night and day? Do they think we want the guilt that comes when the grief is gone?

JUDY: Guilt?

CLARK: Yes! We are guilty. I am selfish.

JUDY: Clark! No! We are not guilty. We are parents. More than that—more than that—we are people.

CLARK *(sitting next to* JUDY*)*: I dream, Judy. When I lie in bed at night, all night, awake. I wonder, what it would be like . . . (Pause.)

JUDY: What it would be like?

CLARK: If we were young again. Very young. In my dream we have time, freedom.

JUDY *(transformed)*: Like a melody . . . like notes in a scale?

CLARK: Yes, like notes in a scale. A bass clef and a treble clef. Playing off one another. Harmonious. Judy!

JUDY: It's all right.

(Lights black out on edge of stage; JUDY *and* CLARK *exit right. Dim, faintly flickering light comes on in* JOSEPH*'s office.* JOSEPH *is asleep in his chair. He dreams.)*

Interlude Six

(Spot downstage right on LITTLE BOY *and* LITTLE GIRL, *rolling rubber ball back and forth.)*

LITTLE GIRL: I think Judy . . .

LITTLE BOY: I think Clark . . .

LITTLE GIRL: I don't believe . . .

LITTLE BOY: I rather tend to . . .

LITTLE GIRL: Well, I think . . .

*(*LITTLE GIRL *and* LITTLE BOY *melt away, leaving* JOSEPH *in his dream.)*

SCENE TWELVE

JOSEPH: And what do you think, Lisa? What do you . . . ? Oh. *(He is awake now.)* I was dreaming about something. Damn. What was it? An old man's memory. An old man's dream.

(Lights brighten also on kitchen. Music—snatches or mutations of The Moonlight Sonata—*is heard as* JOSEPH *recounts his dream.)*

JOSEPH: I was in a room. A small, yellow room. No doors. Just a window, a one-way window, so that everybody could watch me. My side of the window was a mirror. I had to watch myself.

(JUDY and CLARK enter kitchen left, holding hands.)

JUDY: Home again, home again. And I could use a drink.

CLARK: At your service, madame. A martini?

JOSEPH: The walls were plastered with photos of missing children from the "unresolved case" drawer. Names were scrawled across the pictures in blood: Cindy. Christopher. Jenny.

CLARK: How do you feel, honey?

JUDY: It's spring!

JOSEPH: Sarah, my high school sweetheart, was standing in one corner of the room. She was wearing an enormous wedding ring —could hardly pick up her hand. Married my best friend, Jerry. She had this stack of pictures of their kids. So many kids. She held each one up for me to see. "And this one could have been *ours,*" she was saying. "And this one . . ."

(JUDY and CLARK enter living room. CLARK pours drinks. JUDY, carrying a bunch of forsythia and lilacs, dumps out an old, dead flower arrangement and puts the fresh flowers in the vase.)

JUDY: The little green buds on the trees, the fresh scent in the breeze.

JOSEPH: In another corner of the room there was a group of Lisa's friends, crying. The chief was standing in the third corner, counting unsold tickets to the Policeman's Ball. There was a public boycott, he told me.

CLARK (*crossing to piano, bringing drinks*): A toast, my dear?

JOSEPH: I looked at the fourth corner. It was empty.

CLARK: To us. To the two of us.

JOSEPH: I sat in the middle of the yellow box. And on my lap sat Lisa, because . . .

JUDY: To us. Together. (CLARK *drinks, then holds the glass for* JUDY *to drink while she plays.*)

JOSEPH: I found her!

LISA (*illuminated somewhere onstage between* JOSEPH *and* JUDY *and* CLARK): Mommy! Daddy! I'm here!

(*Music stops.* JUDY *and* CLARK *look up, freeze, illuminated by spot. Another spot illuminates* JOSEPH. *He wants to scream, act, unite the* AMORYS. *Sways with energy.*)

JOSEPH: And what will you do, Judy and Clark?

CLARK: To us.

JUDY: Together.

LISA: Mommy! Daddy!

JOSEPH: I found you!

CLARK: Together.

JOSEPH: What . . . ?

JUDY: To—

LISA: Mommy!

CLARK: Us.

LISA: Daddy!

JOSEPH: Wait! That's it. That's the moment.

(JOSEPH still sways—with restraint. Tableau. Spot blacks out on LISA, *then on* JUDY *and* CLARK.*)*

Interlude Seven

(Still spot on JOSEPH. *Spot on* LITTLE BOY *and* LITTLE GIRL, *who are standing on either side of the large yellow box with open lid.)*

LITTLE BOY: What did they do?

LITTLE GIRL: What?

LITTLE BOY: Simple.

LITTLE GIRL: Simple?

LITTLE BOY: Quite simple.

LITTLE GIRL: Quite simple.

LITTLE BOY: They

LITTLE GIRL: Did

LITTLE BOY: What

LITTLE GIRL: Any

LITTLE BOY and LITTLE GIRL: Loving Parents

LITTLE BOY: Would

LITTLE GIRL: Have

LITTLE BOY: Done.

(LITTLE GIRL and LITTLE BOY slam the lid of the yellow box shut, which blacks out the spotlight on JOSEPH. They sit on the box, their backs to the audience. Blackout. Curtain.)

(The Moonlight Sonata is played delicately as the actors take their bows.

ELIZABETH HIRSCHHORN

I thrive on the extremes of theater: the Very Alone stage where I'm hanging out primarily with semideveloped characters and a pen, and the Social Stage, where every moment is spent laughing and fighting, eating and drinking, hating and loving people who have as much of an exaggerated sense of the importance of an ideal production as I do.

I have written and directed plays in sixth, eighth, and twelfth grades. *Sonata,* my third play, was produced at the Playwrights Horizons theater during the 1985 Young Playwrights Festival and then done as a reading, which I codirected during the 1985 First International Festival of Young Playwrights in Sydney, Australia.

I'm a freshman at Harvard College now and had decided to take a break from theater here to explore the *new.* I went to a talk given by a famous playwright the other day, though, and was reminded—by a wave of anxious panic—that it's been too long: theater is somewhat like a drug, and I'm ready for some more.

ABOUT THE PLAY

If I could describe well what I think *Sonata* is about, I might not have written the play. I will say that when I was little my father had a running "joke" that if I didn't exist he could buy one-half of a forty-nine-foot yacht.

ABOUT THE PRODUCTION

My favorite part of the Festival—aside from the bliss of escaping junior year at prep school on my own for six weeks of adventure in New York City—was the opportunity to discover for my-self what a playwright *does* after the original script is written. The Festival was constructed to be noncondescending to the young, inexperienced playwright: I was accepted and allowed to make of casting and rehearsals what I wanted. I chose to delve into every facet of the production. I loved the "reality" of it. I learned to know my own vision of the play and keep it in mind when five people suggested conflicting rewrites. I wish I'd had confidence early in the production to assert my insecurity about the play's set: its gliding platforms eventually encumbered the necessary flow of *Sonata*'s successive Scenes and Interludes.

The people—my creative and patient director, Shelly Raffle, and the actors, dramaturg, and others—made for the exciting and somewhat bizarre social dynamic of the Festival. I learned as much from them as from the process.

The Festival was wonderfully intense. I hope it opens up the same world of possibilities for other Young Playwrights as it did for me.

FIELD DAY

BY LESLIE KAUFMAN
(age eighteen when play was written)
New York, New York

NOTE:
For the purpose of publication in this collection, certain words
have been changed by the playwright and some profanity has
been deleted from the working script of the play as performed at
Playwrights Horizons, New York City, April 7 through April 28,
1985.

CHARACTERS

#1
#2

Scattered about the outskirts of the stage are small pebbles that form a ring that the actors never leave. In the center of the stage is a large rock. Everything on the stage—the walls, the floor, the rock, the costumes—should be made to reflect and thus look the color of the stage light. The stage light will start at a dark purple and will continue to get lighter with appropriate flashes of color. The "soldiers" should be in civilian costume, dressed maybe as if going to a cocktail party, though each should have a style that reflects his character. They will wear boots and helmets and bits of camouflage.

#2: You okay?

(Pause.)

#2: Are you all right?

(Pause.)

#1: No.

#2: No? What's wrong, are you hurt?

#1: Yes.

#2 *(kneeling over #1):* Where are you hurt, where does it hurt?

#1: Everywhere.

#2: Do you think you hurt your back when you fell?

(Pause.)

#1: It is not my back that is hurt.

#2: How do ya know, where does it hurt?

#1: I'm bleeding.

#2: I don't see any blood. I don't see any blood.

#1 *(insistent):* I'm bleeding all over.

#2 *(searching frantically):* I don't see any blood. Tell me where it hurts, where is it coming from?

#1 *(almost hysterical):* All over. It is gushing out of me, I am bleeding to death, I am bleeding.

#2: You're not bleeding, there is no blood.

#1: I am in pain.

#2: But you are not bleeding.

#1: All right, I am not bleeding, but I am in pain.

#2: I don't even think you're hurt.

#1 *(hysterical):* I'm hurt, I'm in pain, I'm bleeding.

#2: You're just panicking.

#1: I've already panicked.

#2: There is no reason to panic. Our position is excellent. We landed in the minefield. We can't be ten minutes from our target. *(Pause.)* I'm sure we haven't been sighted. They wouldn't think we'd land in a minefield.

#1: No, who would?

#2 *(pleased):* Pretty clever.

#1: Pretty clever. Pretty clever of us to drop like pieces of the night into a minefield. Deep in enemy territory. What a clever plan.

(Pause.)

#2: Are you being sarcastic? *(Pause.)* Just remember we're here on an important mission, we have a purpose. *(Pause.)* Well, we haven't been sighted so we will just wait here. *(Settles himself in, looks around. With spirit.)* It feels good. It is going to be a good day.

#1: It feels good—the air, the sun, the dawn.

#2: No, no, the mission. The mission feels good. *(Looking up.)* What do you think about the weather?

#1: I think there will be some.

#2 *(makes a face):* I think we're even going to get good weather.

#1: As long as we are having weather, it is good.

#2: What time do ya think it will be dark again?

#1: When the sun rises it will be light, when it sets it will be dark.

#2: The sun isn't supposed to set until seven fourteen P.M. Now, normally we couldn't leave until hours after that, but with this cloud cover it will be dark enough, say we plan to leave at eight. *(Pause.)* What do ya think?

(Pause.)

#1: I am not going.

#2: Of course you are, you're just scared a little.

#1: Not just a little.

#2: It's okay to be scared—you'll get over it. Besides, we're behind enemy territory. What else would you do?

#1: I don't know. I am thinking about it.

#2: Don't think, just relax. That's an order. Now we've got fourteen hours to go before we leave, so get comfortable.

#1: I am comfortable, and I'm not going.

#2: We've got quite a wait. *(Pause.)* Let's talk!

#1: Let's.

#2: What about back home?

#1: What about it?

#2 *(dreamily):* Well, sometimes I think I just can't go on fighting, then I think of all the things I care for back home.

#1 *(interrupting):* And the draft board.

#2 *(laughing):* And the draft board. But knowing I am protecting my mother, my farm, my younger brother, and his pet frog. I feel like even though it is hell I can stand it.

#1 *(Nods.)*

#2: What I miss most is waking up in my own bed with clean sheets, looking out my window and seeing the sun rise over the field and then smelling the bacon frying, fresh bacon from our own pigs.

(Pause.)

#1: Who is frying the bacon?

#2: My mom. She always gets up to make us breakfast.

#1: She gets up before dawn to fry your bacon? Crazy lady.

#2 *(ignoring #1):* She is one hell of a woman—never selfish, always caring.

#1: Yes. *(Pause.)* Is she happy? That is, getting up at five thirty in the morning and making your breakfast.

#2: Happiest lady around, always smiling, everybody loves Mom.

#1: How do you know?

#2: Here, I have a picture of her. *(Reaches into his pocket.)* I always carry it with me it brings me good luck. *(Opens wallet, shows picture.)* See there she is.

#1 *(Nods.)*

#2 *(flipping through pictures):* See this one—pretty, ain't she?

#1 *(Nods.)*

#2: She's my girl. Soft as a rose. I'd take the pickup truck, and we'd screw around in the back. I loved the way she felt. What I miss most was her hair, really soft and blond. *(Pause.)* What about you, do you have a girl?

#1 *(Nods.)*

#2: What do you miss most about her?

#1: The way she sweats. *(Pause. Then, almost angry.)* Her hair is kinda greasy, but boy can she sweat. She has got tight little thighs, and I have to stay on top of her and ram myself into her. Like I am being squashed to death. And she sweats, and our bodies stick together, and then as I am going in and out, the sweat pools slosh off her body and onto the bed. In the summer the heat is so intense that making love is almost like suffocating. The stink is almost too much to bear, and then it is over, and we lie like pigs in a pool of greasy sweat. *(Pause. #2 is very uncomfortable. #1 is over his anger, but says as a retort:)* When this is all over maybe we should get together sometime and go on a double date. *(#2 is still uncomfortable.)* What about back home?

#2 *(confused, anxious):* What about it?

#1 *(evasive):* Oh, nothing.

(Pause.)

#2: Do you miss anything about your home?

#1: Holes in the road. Big craters. After it rains, the craters are filled with water. I like to climb into them and just sit in the rain water.

#2: You're doing this because you like to sit in holes in the road?

#1: No. I don't know why I am doing this.

(Pause.)

#2: Well, ours is not to question.

(Pause.)

#1: Why?

#2: Why what?

#1: Why is ours not to question?

#2: What do ya mean?

#1: What do you think I mean?

#2: I dunno, what da ya mean?

#1: I mean, what do you mean by the statement, "Ours is not to question"?

#2: It is not our right to question. In a time of war we must trust our superiors. Nothing would get done if we didn't.

(Pause.)

#1: Why?

#2: Why what?

#1: Why in a time of war must we trust our superiors? Why wouldn't they get . . .

#2 *(interrupting):* Cut it out, will you? Just stop it. You know this is the way it has to be. Don't start this again. Just stop it. Stop it right now!

(Pause.)

#1: Why?

#2 *(unbelievingly):* Why what?

#1: Why stop now?

#2 *(throws his hand up in exasperation and walks away. Pause . . . wait. He walks back angrily.)*

#2: I thought you lived in a city?

#1: I did.

#2: You said you sat in the potholes after it rained, so you must be from the country.

#1: Cities have potholes.

#2: Yeah, but no one sits in potholes in city streets. It is dirty and dangerous. *(Triumphant.) They* wouldn't let you.

#1: *They* let me.

#2: Who let you?

#1: *They.*

#2: *They* who?

#1: The *they* that wasn't supposed to let me.

#2 *(walks away again, comes back):* Look, tensions are high. Face it, this is a high-pressure situation we are in here. It is understandable that we are both a little nervous about this mission.

#1: I feel like we have been dating for years and are having our first fight.

#2: As I was saying, it is okay to be nervous.

#1: I'm not nervous.

#2: What? Not ten minutes ago you said you were scared.

#1: That was before I knew that I wasn't going.

#2: Oh, you're not starting this again, are you?

#1: I'm not starting anything. *(Pause.)* I am just not going.

#2: I wish you wouldn't play these games.

#1: I am tired of playing games. That is why I am not going.

#2: What does this have to do with playing games? *(Pause.)* How come I don't understand what you're saying?

#1: I dunno. How come?

#2 *(angry):* You know, there are an awful lot of things you don't know?

#1: I know.

(Pause.)

#2: I am getting tired.

#1: Sleep.

#2: Want something to eat?

#1: What do you have?

#2: You know what I have. You packed.

#1: Tell me anyway. Unpack and look through everything and tell me. *(Pause.)* I'll pretend to be surprised.

#2 *(looking through rations bag):* We have some apples.

#1 *(looking over his shoulder):* Any veal?

#2: And a canteen of water.

#1: I just love a picnic.

#2: So you want an apple?

#1: No.

(#2 bites his apple. Crunching sound heard. He munches away. #1 watches deliberately.)

#1: How far do you think the sound of apple carries?

#2 *(confused):* I dunno.

#1: What are the odds they have equipment sensitive enough to pick up minute sounds, like an apple crunching?

#2: They don't have equipment like that, do they?

#1: Who are they? *(Pause.)* Lips smacking.

#2: What?

#1: No one can hear veal being chewed—that is, if it is tender veal, cooked properly. All they could hear would be lips smacking. And people smack their lips for, oh *(pause),* so many reasons.

#2 *(looking at apple):* Do you think I should get rid of it?

(#1 nods. #2 throws apple behind him. There is a pause and a deafening sound as a mine explodes.)

#1: Do you think they have sound equipment sensitive enough to pick that up?

#2: Get down, will you? Just get down! I forgot, I completely forgot we are in a minefield.

#1: Still are, no thanks to you.

#2: I am sorry, so sorry, I may have blown the entire mission.

#1: We should have eaten the veal.

#2 *(mildly incoherent, apparently shocked):* Oh, okay, okay, come on, get ahold of yourself. We gotta think quick, they must have heard that.

#1: Who's they?

#2: They'll probably come to investigate *(Packing.)* Though they may not—we can't take the chance. Look, I think we'll be at less of a risk if we start now. I mean, sitting here we're just dead ducks.

(Pause; #1 just stares with incredulity.)
I realize this is a big change of plans but as leader of this mission, I feel that the enemy could be fast approaching.

(#1 looks around and then looks at #2 with disbelief.)
I think we have no choice but to get the hell out of here. We'll just continue with the mission as planned. Come on, let's go!

#1: I am not going.

#2: Don't start this again.

#1: I am not starting anything. *(Pause).* I am just not going.

#2: Not going? You haven't even thought about what this means! We are miles behind enemy lines in a minefield—what are you going to do, hang out?

#1: I am thinking about it.

#2: Great. Better to stay here in a minefield waiting to be captured and tortured by the enemy, or be blown up than to do our job and get out of here.

#1 *(stares in disbelief):* It is amazing how much comprehension you don't have of our situation.

#2: Look, I'm not pretending it's easy. Maybe it is difficult. Maybe it is impossible.

#1: Maybe. Maybe.

#2: Maybe it is even suicidal, but it is what we have been trained to do. We don't have many other choices right now. Besides, are you telling me it is better to wait here helpless like rodents in a mousetrap we've made for ourselves than at least die in the service of our country with a little dignity?

#1: I am not dying knowing that there is some sergeant at HQ laughing at me for believing blindly to the end.

(Pause.)

#2: You knew this was a dangerous mission from the start. Why did you wait until now to quit the army?

#1: They tricked me. I was tricked. There, dangerous is a medal, lots of applause, all in the line of duty. Here, dangerous is

suicidal. I am quitting now because now is the last chance I have
to quit.

(Pause.)

#2: Look, you're thinking about this too much. Just stop think-
ing, and let's do what we've been trained to do. You'll see it will
be easy. *(Pause.)* A lot easier than what we're doing here now.

#1: I'll stop thinking.

#2: Good. Come on, let's go.

#1: I am not going.

#2: Stop it!

(Deafening explosion as a mine goes off.)

#1: Are you all right?

(Pause.)

#2: Hey, you all right?

#1 *(weakly):* No.

#2: Are you really bleeding?

#1: I'm being bled.

#2: I don't see any blood.

#1: There is blood.

#2: Where, if there is blood, where is it?

#1 *(screams in pain hysterically):* I'm in pain, I'm in pain.

#2 *(louder):* Stop it, stop it! You're being crazy.

#1: I'm crazy, I'm crazy, I'm in pain.

#2: Stop it, stop it! I'm not going to let you do this. You can't do this to me. We can't stay here, we'll get our brains blown out for sure. I'm not going to sit here. I'm not going to stay here. We've got a mission to accomplish, it is our only way out. We've got to take it! *(Grabs* #1.) Are you listening to me? *(Shakes* #1.) Listen! Listen to me, I'm not going to let you kill me. We gotta go. You're coming if I have to drag you all the way. If I have to, I'll carry you all the way there and do your job for you, but I am going to make you come.

#1: If you're doing my job for me, why do I have to come?

#2: Because you do. Because I have to. Because if I am going, you are going, too. Because it is your duty, and I am never going to let you get out of it, not even at the last minute we ever have! Because you're copping out. Because you're killing me. Forget your responsibility to them—you have a responsibility to me. And I am not going to let you kill me! *(Pause.)* Get up and start moving! *(Pause.)* Did you hear me? *Move!*

(#1 stares incredulously.)
We are just going to go ahead with the plan HQ made, and we are going now.

#1: Why now?

#2: Because if they didn't hear the first mine, they heard the second, and they are sure to be suspicious, so let's get the hell out of here.

#1: How are we going to do that?

#2: What do ya mean?

#1: What do you think I mean?

#2: We are going to walk.

#1: We are going to walk through a live minefield?

(Pause.)

#2: You okay?

(Pause.)

#1: You all right?

#2: I'm bleeding.

(Curtain.)

LESLIE KAUFMAN

I was born in New York City and grew up in Greenwich Village. I graduated from Stuyvesant High School and now attend Stanford University.

ABOUT THE PLAY

The idea for *Field Day* grew out of a bit of dialogue I wrote in a playwriting class in my senior year of high school. The dialogue had been read out loud and had received a positive response from my classmates, so I developed it, on a whim really, into a play during the next two weeks. I handed it in to my teacher and didn't think about it again until it won first place in the NYC Young Playwrights Festival. It was then entered automatically into the national competition, which it won during my freshman year at Stanford.

I must admit that my feelings about having the play produced were very ambivalent. I was ecstatic about the honor of being chosen and about the opportunities being offered to me. However, after I heard the play read out loud for the first time, I realized that my conception of my writing had been completely internal and that I had never really imagined, except in the vaguest way, what it would be like produced. Hearing the words I had written spoken publicly to a large group of people made me feel terribly exposed and stupid. I began to hate what I had written, and no reassuring from actors, directors, or producers could make me like it.

When the show was playing Off Broadway I would sit in the theater, in the back, hide my head behind the shoulder of some friend or relative, and cringe with each line. My poor director thought I had been disappointed with his interpretation of the play, but in truth it was just the publicness of it all that scared me.

THE GROUND ZERO CLUB

BY CHARLIE SCHULMAN
(age eighteen when play was written)
New York, New York

NOTE:
For the purpose of publication in this collection, certain words have been changed by the playwright and some profanity has been deleted from the working script of the play as performed at Playwrights Horizons in New York City, April 7 through April 28, 1985.

CHARACTERS

SECURITY GUARD
VOICEOVER
TOURIST
SAL ID, a twenty-five-year-old, over-the-hill punk
   rocker
ANGELA, his Catholic school girlfriend
BOB
FEONNA
TANYA, an antinuclear activist

TIME: later tonight
PLACE: the observation deck of the Empire State
   Building

The set is on two levels that divide the stage in half. Downstage is the outside viewing area. Downstage right is a viewer telescope, which requires a quarter to operate. Four stairs lead up to the raised half upstage, which is inside the observation deck. Inside stage left a corner of the souvenir stand can be seen. Upstage left is a public telephone hanging on a side wall. In between the stand and the telephone is the only entrance/exit. A backdrop of New York City at night surrounds the stage. The backdrop may be a drawing, a photograph, or a cut-out, as long as a feeling of looking down on the city is conveyed. Hovering over the stage is a red, white, and blue glow that emanates from the top of the building.

Staring through the viewer telescope at individual members of the audience is the TOURIST. *The faint sounds of sirens, car horns, and general panic in the streets can be heard as searchlights scan the sky and stage. In the midst of this confusion, the disheveled figure of the* SECURITY GUARD *can be seen bursting through the door and down the steps. Loud static can be heard coming from the walkie-talkie that he holds in front of him. As he looks over the side and into the street below, the lights slowly come up.*

GUARD (*screaming into the walkie-talkie*): What do you mean, nobody can do anything about it?

VOICEOVER: Sorry, Jack, it's a nuclear war. Yes, nuclear war!

GUARD: What?

VOICEOVER: Yes, nuclear war!

GUARD: What am I supposed to do now?

VOICEOVER: You can take the rest of the day off.

GUARD: I'd rather have the overtime.

VOICEOVER: Okay. *(Static is heard.)*

GUARD: So what do we do now? I've never seen so many people down there. Traffic is not moving at all. Who knows the emergency plan to get out of this city? Did they say it on the radio? What's a guy supposed to do during a nuclear war, anyway? All I did was go to the bathroom, and when I got out, all this was going on, and everyone had left—even Marcie, who runs the souvenir stand. She probably wanted to be with her boyfriend. *(He takes a sip from his flask.)* So I'm the one who winds up feeling stupid for having noplace to go. I wish I had someone I was close to. There's my mother, of course, but she lives down in Florida. *(Static is heard.)* Hello! *(More static. He turns off the walkie-talkie and returns it to his belt. He runs back inside to the public telephone and dials a number.)* Three dollars and fifty cents? *(He searches his pockets, then drops the receiver and climbs over the souvenir stand.)* Marcie, you cleared out the register. *(He climbs back over and picks up the receiver.)* Yeah, operator, I would like to make a collect call to Florida. My name is Jack. Hello, Mom, it's Jack. *(Bursting into tears.)* I can't believe this is happening but I love you, Ma, I love you. *(Suddenly he stops crying.)* What do you mean, you won't accept the charges? I don't have any money on me. How can I visit you? I live in New York! Ma!

(They have been disconnected. He hangs up the phone, walks over to the window that separates the inside from the outside, presses his face up against the glass, and begins to cry. SAL ID and ANGELA enter. SAL is pulling ANGELA, who is resisting, by the wrist. SAL sports a sleeveless T-shirt with a picture of his dead hero, Sid Vicious. ANGELA is quite a bit smarter than her loser boyfriend. She bites SAL on the arm.)

SAL: Ahhhhh!
(ANGELA exits. SAL follows her, muttering under his breath. They reenter, SAL carrying ANGELA under his arm.)

ANGELA: Let go of me, you bastard! Get your hands off of me!

(SAL puts his hand over her mouth.)

SAL: We're the first ones here! *(Fiendishly.)* Lucky we were in the neighborhood.

ANGELA: Why did you bring me here? This place is for tourists!

SAL: Don't be stupid, Angela. You heard what they said on the radio, just like I did.

ANGELA *(looking over the side):* You can't just leave the car like that in the middle of the street with the keys in the ignition.

SAL: We don't need it anymore.

ANGELA: Let's go home, Sal, please? Let's go back to Astoria.

SAL: Forget it. We'd never make it back past the Fifty-Ninth Street Bridge, and even if we did make it back, what good would it do us? Maybe something will go wrong, and they'll blow up New Jersey instead. Wouldn't that be great? No more bridge-and-tunnel traffic crowding up the bars!

(The GUARD selects a postcard from the souvenir stand and presses it up against the window.)

ANGELA: If we went back, we could say good-bye to everyone. I want to see my mother. We should be with the people who care about us.

GUARD *(writing on the postcard):* Dear Anybody.

SAL: What difference does it make? Look, Angela, we are with the people who care about us—we're with each other. I don't want to go back there. I've been spending my whole life trying to get out of that place.

ANGELA: In that case you haven't done very well.

SAL: I'm not there now, am I? That's the great thing about this country. You can blow up anywhere you like. They don't have that kind of freedom in Russia.

ANGELA: I once heard that if you were up here and dropped a penny over the side, it would make a three-inch hole in the pavement. I wonder if it's true? *(She drops a penny over the side.)*

SAL: Don't you know where you are, Angela? This is ground zero. This is the spot where all those missiles are aimed at. Maybe we'll get a good look at one. *(Looking around.)* The observation deck of the Empire State Building. Believe me, Angela, this is the best place to be at a time like this. We're lucky—we're going to see the last that anyone does of this town. So enjoy the view while it's still there. *(They both look out at the city.)* You know, I've never told you this before, but I'm a member of the Ground Zero Club.

ANGELA: What are you talking about? You never belonged to anything before.

SAL: Well, I belong to something now. All the members are supposed to meet here right before a nuclear war to join together for one last tremendous party. I'm sure the rest of the members will be getting here soon. I sure have waited a long time for this.

ANGELA: I don't believe this is happening. I never asked for this. It's not fair. I haven't had any fun yet. I haven't enjoyed anything at all yet. I was just about to become happy. It would probably have started tomorrow.

SAL: It's just like the seventh game of the World Series, when the announcer says, "There is no tomorrow." I get such a kick out of hearing them say that.

ANGELA: All I ever asked for was a dishwasher and a house to put it in, with children who would take turns loading it.

SAL: Yeah, I was really looking forward to that, but there's no point in dreaming.

ANGELA: We could have had so much together. Another ten years, and we would have been able to move out of my parents' home. Of course, you're screwed up now, but you would have straightened out.

SAL: We're better off this way. We would probably have gotten divorced in a few years anyhow. What if the kids turned out to be jerks who had terrible personalities and were addicted to drugs like I am? What would we have done then? One day we would have come home and found them with all these electrodes hooked up to their brains. I woulda hadda said, "Kids you don't need to get high with a computer. In our day we just smoked pot and ate Quaaludes."

ANGELA: You're wrong, Sal. Our children won't get high from computers. They'll the same drugs that we did. We'll have plenty of liquor around the house, so there won't be any need for computers.

GUARD *(writing):* I am up here on the observation deck. If you are as lonely as I am and have no one to be with during this nuclear war, then you should come up to the top so that we can spend our last moments together.

ANGELA: How much time do you think we have left?

SAL: Who knows? Maybe ten, fifteen minutes.

GUARD: Sincerely, a concerned citizen.

SAL: But a lot of things can still happen if we make every second count and fill our time with intensely profound revelations. I'm good at those when the pressure is on.

(The GUARD drops the postcard over the side.)

ANGELA: Oh, no! The seconds are just passing by, and I'm not having any revelations. What are we going to do? We can't just stand here. I mean, should we pray or what?

GUARD: What's the point in praying? The human race is committing suicide. Nobody goes to heaven.

ANGELA: I'm not committing suicide. I didn't put those missiles there. I never wanted a nuclear war.

SAL: Don't worry, baby. Hell might be a terrible place, but it's probably better than your parents' house. I'm sure we'll be able to find a nice neighborhood. Yeah, I'll get a job, we'll buy a mobile home, raise a family—it'll be just like life, only much more horrible. Burning for eternity couldn't be as bad as it sounds. I'm sure you just pass out after a few minutes, anyway.

ANGELA: Maybe the radio made a mistake! It doesn't feel like there isn't any time left. If we really only had twenty minutes to live, I'm certain I wouldn't be doing what I'm doing right now.

SAL: What would you be doing?

ANGELA: Something wild and exciting. I wouldn't still be planning for the future. I would never be here if this was really happening.

(The sound of the viewer telescope running out of time can be heard. The TOURIST *looks up for a moment, puts a quarter into the machine, and resumes looking at the audience.)*

SAL *(to the* GUARD*)*: Hi, mister, glad you could make it. It just seems right that we spend our last few minutes with a total stranger. *(To* ANGELA.*)* What is it that your mother always says?

ANGELA *(reluctantly)*: "The best friends you'll ever have are the people you were forced to be with."

SAL: Ain't that the truth? *(The* GUARD *takes a sip from his flask.)* I'm Sal Id. You might have heard of me or seen my band, Violent Apathy.

GUARD: I don't think so. Where have you played?

SAL: We had a few gigs down at the . . . *(Pauses to think for a moment.)* But they closed it down and turned it into a gay men's roller disco. We also gigged at the . . . *(He thinks for a mo-*

ment.) But now it's one of those fancy cheese and pasta shops. Actually, we don't play together anymore.

ANGELA: They had a vicious argument because nobody cared about the band.

(*The* GUARD *passes his flask to* SAL.)

SAL: This is my girlfriend, Angela.

GUARD: It certainly is a pleasure to die with you two.

ANGELA: You mean it's definite? Maybe they made a mistake.

GUARD: Not likely. At least, everybody down there doesn't seem to think so. They're all rushing to something or other. It's too bad it takes a nuclear war to make some of these people do what they've always wanted to do.

SAL: That's what's so terrific about it. Things that we've always wanted to do but couldn't for whatever reason, we can do right now.

(*They all stand in silence for ten seconds, not doing anything.*)
Isn't it a great feeling?

ANGELA: It's kind of hard to think about my own death when I haven't even gotten over John Lennon's yet.

SAL: I'm sick and tired of hearing about how wonderful John Lennon was! It's easy to want everyone to love each other when you have three hundred million dollars. Sid Vicious, on the other hand (*pointing to his shirt*)—now, Sid was the real thing. He never placed himself above the scum that came to see him play. He was a real working-class hero. Didn't let being famous make him look like some kind of great guy. In fact, as he got more famous, he became more messed up on purpose, just to prove that being a star was nothing but a bunch of bullshit.

GUARD: You've got a real good sense of humor, kid. How do you like that? Just when you think it's all over, you find a new friend.

(They shake hands and share the bottle. BOB *and* FEONNA *appear inside. They have been on an expensive night on the town.* BOB *is wearing a tuxedo, and* FEONNA *a silver lamé jumpsuit.)*

BOB *(to* FEONNA): Are you certain you want to come here? I have pull at Windows on the World. I'm sure we could get a table there.

FEONNA: No, no, no, absolutely not. This is the more appropriate place to die.

BOB: I wonder how things will be after this is all over?

FEONNA: Exactly like that "after the nuclear holocaust" party we went to last Friday. Remember when we asked for ice to put in our drinks?

BOB: Wasn't that terrific? *(He laughs.)* "No ice," they said. "There will be no ice after the bomb." What a thing to think of. No ice. *(Laughing.)* Hard to imagine, really.

ANGELA: You know, maybe this isn't the safest place to be right now.

GUARD *(to* SAL*):* If you ever need someone to talk to, you can come to me.

SAL: Thanks, that's real nice of you.

ANGELA: I know the view is great, but maybe we'd have a better chance if we were somewhere else.

BOB: We can still go to Windows.

FEONNA: Are you insane? Do you realize how difficult it will be to get a cab?

SAL: To tell the truth, I sort of do have a problem.

GUARD: Nothing too heavy, if you know what I mean? Nothing monumental. Little things, trivial things, if you can get at what I'm saying.

SAL: She's pregnant.

GUARD: I was just making a gesture, damn it! I don't want to hear your problems. I was just being a nice guy.

SAL: Yeah. You know, I'm feeling kind of guilty. I would have married her. I would have done the right thing. Lucky it didn't have to come to that, though.

ANGELA: Maybe we should go underground, Sal.

SAL: Why would you want to do that?

(SAL and ANGELA continue talking as the GUARD looks on. The door swings open, and FEONNA walks outside, followed by BOB.)

FEONNA: I see no reason why I shouldn't jump from here. This is as good a place as any—even better.

BOB: All I'm saying is that the Twin Towers are a bit higher, that's all, dear. And they have a bar.

FEONNA: Out of my way. I'm going to jump. Good-bye, Bob.

(She makes a move to jump over the side, but the GUARD stops her.)

GUARD: I'm sorry, ma'am, but I can't let you do that.

FEONNA: Why not?

BOB: Let go of my wife.

FEONNA: Give him some money, Bob.

(BOB *gives him fifty dollars.*)

BOB: What's the matter? Fifty isn't enough?

GUARD: You want to pay me so your wife can kill herself?

BOB: Of course I don't want to pay you, but it doesn't look as if I have a choice, does it?

(*The sound of the viewer telescope running out of time can be heard. The* TOURIST *looks up, takes a quarter out of his pocket, puts it into the machine, and resumes looking through the viewer.*)

GUARD: But she's your wife! Don't you want to spend these last moments together so you can comfort each other?

BOB: Look, we weren't born together, we didn't travel together, so I see no reason why we should ruin it all by dying together.

FEONNA: Why shouldn't I die the way I want to instead of the way somebody else wants me to? I find this whole nuclear issue so distasteful that, frankly, I don't wish to have any part of it. All people ever talk about is nuclear war, nuclear war, nuclear war. Even after they had that TV movie, people were still talking about it. It's just so passé.

SAL: That movie was great. I was hoping they would turn it into, like, a weekly series out of it.

FEONNA: But today was the final straw. There we were, celebrating Bob's new appointment, when this man came running into the restaurant with this vulgar news.

GUARD (*to* BOB): What kind of appointment, Bob?

BOB: Oh, it's nothing, really.

FEONNA: Don't be silly, Bobby. A government position in Washington is not nothing at all.

SAL: What kind of position?

FEONNA: Bob is the new assistant secretary to the associate secretary of the secretary to the secretary of defense.

ANGELA: Secretary of defense? What are you doing here? You should be trying to do something to stop this.

BOB: I don't officially take office until Monday.

FEONNA *(to the* GUARD*):* Why don't you be a nice man and let go of my arm before my husband sees to it that you never work in this town again?

(The GUARD *backs off.)*

SAL *(embracing* ANGELA*):* Oh, Angie, this is turning out better than I ever thought it would. Everybody dies together, and nobody has to miss a thing. Finally some justice—everyone suffers equally. Can you believe it? *Me* and the assistant secretary to the associate secretary of the secretary to the secretary of defense at the same time in the same place? This is unbelievable. This could only happen in America.

(TANYA appears inside. She is holding a box of buttons in one hand and a postcard in the other. She peers out at the rest of the people, in search of someone.)

ANGELA: Maybe we shouldn't just give up and die, Sal.

TANYA: Get your buttons here! All antinuclear paraphernalia half off. Clearance sale—everything must go!

FEONNA: Oh, Bob, a sale!

TANYA: Better active today than radioactive tomorrow!

SAL: Oh, come off it. Some people never know when to give up and relax.

TANYA: At least I did my best. Now I'll try and raise consciousness until the end.

(The sound of the viewer telescope running down can be heard. The TOURIST *looks up, puts another quarter in the machine, and resumes looking at the audience.)*

BOB *(to* FEONNA*):* What's the matter, dear? Why don't you jump?

FEONNA: Aren't you going to stop me?

BOB: Why would you do that if this is what you want? You know I always try to make you happy.

FEONNA: My analyst would have tried to stop me.

BOB: What could he do for you? The man broke down and cried when he saw Freud's couch on a visit to Vienna.

SAL: Wasn't that the guy who wanted to kill his father and sleep with his mother? I never wanted to do that.

TANYA *(shouting over everybody):* It's time for everybody to face up to the fact that they saw this coming and didn't do anything about it.

SAL: I always wanted to kill my father and my mother and then sleep with both of them.

BOB *(to* TANYA*):* The human race was out of control a long time ago. It's a good thing this is happening now, before we did something really terrible.

TANYA: Don't you see that you are all responsible for this?

ANGELA: What about him? He's a politician.

BOB: Don't look at me—I'm just a cog in the wheel.

ANGELA *(to* TANYA*):* He was just appointed to something really big today.

TANYA: So you're the new secretary of the secretary to the secretary!

BOB *(backing up):* I don't take office until Monday.

TANYA: Okay, everybody, we got this guy right where we want him.

BOB: I'm innocent, I tell you! *(*SAL, ANGELA, TANYA, *and the* GUARD *circle around* BOB.*)* I wouldn't worry if I were you. I'm sure our government knows what's going on and that they're doing everything in their power to avert a disaster. Why, we're probably speaking with the Russians right now.

FEONNA *(taking out a cigarette):* Bob, I need a light.

BOB: All right! I tried, I really did. We thought we could prevent a confrontation, but I guess I was wrong. Everybody makes mistakes.

(He forces a smile.)

FEONNA *(to the* TOURIST*):* I need a light.

BOB: Of course, somebody has to take responsibility for this and, well, it might as well be me. *(They nod their heads.)* I'm as much responsible for this as anyone. *(They nod again.)*

FEONNA *(throwing the cigarettes over the side):* In that case, I quit.

BOB: I should be punished for this! Really I should! *(All nod as they close in.)* I should be tortured! Someone torture me slowly and painfully. Please! I'll buy all these buttons. How many do you have?

TANYA: About three hundred. (BOB *hands her ten dollars and takes the box. As he picks up the first button, he begins to weep. Slowly he puts every button in the box on his clothing.*)

FEONNA: Bob, I changed my mind. I don't think I wanted to come here after all. Why don't we go home and watch the rest of this on the news?

BOB (*crying and oblivious to* FEONNA *as he looks at the button that he is putting on his collar*): "What if they gave a war and nobody came?"

GUARD (*finishing what is left in his flask*): It's empty. I guess I might as well quit also.

(*He throws the flask over the side.*)

ANGELA: Sal, I think we should break up.

SAL: What are you talking about? You're just upset, that's all.

ANGELA: No, Sal, I don't think you're very good for me.

SAL: You can't do this to me, Angela. We need each other right now. You can't leave me in the middle of a nuclear war!

ANGELA: It's always something with you. If it wasn't a nuclear war, it would be something else.

SAL: Look, we'll discuss this in hell. (*They continue arguing.*)

TANYA: Is there a concerned citizen here?

GUARD: Yes?

TANYA: I got your postcard. (*She holds it up.*)

GUARD: I was hoping you would.

ANGELA: When are you going to get off this rebel punk stuff, huh? You're twenty-five—you're too old to be a punk rocker. Look at yourself. You're growing facial hair.

SAL: What do you want for me to do, sell out? I would if someone was buying.

ANGELA: Look at the way you dress, Sal. You're out of date. Sid is dead, and all that shit is over.

SAL: So what? Who cares? So big deal—I'll never be a big star. So what? Who cares! But let me tell you one thing. It took me a long freakin' time to hit rock bottom, and I'm not going to stop there. *(He takes out a pair of drumsticks from his back pocket and pretends to play the drums.)*
One, two, three, four!

> *"Anarchy burger, hold the government!*
> *Anarchy burger, hold the government*
> *. . . Please!"*

ANGELA: I've known a lot of losers in my life, but you are the most boring.

SAL *(holding a bag of pills):* Yeah? Well, I guess there's no point in saving all these for the weekend. *(He eats them all.)*

BOB *(still crying and looking at another button that he is putting on his clothes):* "War is not healthy for children and other living things!"

FEONNA *(finally realizing that nobody cares whether she jumps or not):* I feel so out of place. I don't have anything in common with these people. This is just like all the parties I go to. I feel so lonely and bored.

GUARD: I know we hardly know each other, and I know it's hard to say "I love you" to a stranger, but I think I really do. You're special. I don't know you, and I never will. *(The GUARD and TANYA begin to kiss.)*

FEONNA *(to* ANGELA*):* Maybe we have something in common. Do you play tennis?

ANGELA: No.

BOB *(still crying and putting on buttons):* "Draft beer not boys!"

*(*TANYA *and the* GUARD *stop kissing.)*

GUARD: What's the matter?

FEONNA *(to* ANGELA*):* Do you like to go horseback riding?

*(*ANGELA *shakes her head.)*

TANYA: I don't know. I just don't feel the same way I used to, that's all.

FEONNA: Wind surfing?

GUARD: Did I do something wrong?

FEONNA *(to* ANGELA*):* Do you have any hobbies?

TANYA: It's just that I'm not quite ready for a relationship at this point of my life. It's not you, it's me. Of course I'm flattered about the way you feel toward me. I just have no time for this right now. It's my work. It's very important to me. I hope you're not taking this personally.

GUARD: Don't worry about me.

*(*ANGELA *starts to cry.)*

FEONNA: Don't cry, honey. Everything is going to be all right.

ANGELA: What do you mean, everything is going to be all right? We're all going to die.

FEONNA: That's what I mean.

ANGELA: I feel like I've wasted my whole life. I never did anything, I never went anywhere.

FEONNA: Don't feel too bad. I went everywhere, and I still didn't do anything.

ANGELA: If only we had some time left, I would get out of Astoria. I would either go to Wilfred Academy to become a beauty practitioner and do some real perming and bleaching, or even better, I would go to college and become a lawyer so I could have some real power and get elected and change everything.

SAL: I hope that everybody here is having a good time. That's what we're here for anyway, and I think it's a great thing that everyone could make it here today. I also think that at this time we should not forget our fellow members who could not be here, for they are here in spirit.

FEONNA: What fellow members?

SAL: The members of the club who couldn't be here for whatever reason. Coming up here was a great idea, and I just want to say that all things considered, this is the best thing that I have ever been a part of.

TANYA: What club?

SAL: The Ground Zero Club! This is the only time we ever met. That's why everybody is here! *(To the GUARD.)* Isn't that why you came?

GUARD: I'm sorry, but I don't think I've ever heard of the Ground Zero Club. I just work here.

SAL *(to BOB, who is still down on his knees sobbing):* What about you? Aren't all you guys in Washington secret members?

BOB *(almost completely covered with buttons):* "Bread not bombs!"

SAL *(to* FEONNA*):* What about you?

FEONNA: Oh, I came here to kill myself, but I changed my mind.

SAL *(pointing at* TANYA*):* You!

TANYA: Me?

SAL: Why did you come here?

TANYA: I came for two reasons. The first one was that I was invited.

(She waves her postcard.)

SAL: By a member of the club?

TANYA: No.

SAL: Oh. What's the other reason?

TANYA: Because I wanted to witness for myself the destruction of the greatest phallic symbol in America.

SAL: Sorry I asked.

ANGELA: How did you hear about this club, Sal?

SAL: I don't remember.

FEONNA: Are you sure that it exists?

SAL: Of course it exists! I don't believe this! Where are all the members?

(Everyone turns their head toward the TOURIST. *The sound of the viewer telescope running out of time can be heard. He looks up from the viewer, takes a quarter out of his pocket, inserts it into the machine, and resumes looking through it.)*

ANGELA: There aren't any. At least, none of them showed up.

SAL *(turning on everybody, like a madman):* What do you mean, none of them showed up? What do you call all you people? You're all members of the club, whether you like it or not! Don't give me no bullshit reasons. I know why you all came here! Because you all want to see this happen! It turns you on, doesn't it? Huh? You get a kinky thrill out of watching everything be blown to smithereens, don't you? Everything has been leading up to this day. We have wanted this for a long, long time! Everybody here can't wait until it's all over.

(The TOURIST motions to the GUARD.)

GUARD: Huh? You want me to have a look? *(He looks through the viewer telescope as the TOURIST motions out toward the city.)* The Statue of Liberty. *(The TOURIST nods his head.)* There she is, the old lady herself. And here it comes! I can see a missile coming straight toward us! These machines are pretty powerful. I wonder who makes them. *(The TOURIST smiles.)* It's getting closer. This is really amazing!

SAL *(in a drug-induced frenzy):* This is it!

TANYA: Remember, the revolution will be after the nuclear holocaust!

(The machine turns itself off.)

GUARD: Son of a bitch! Does anybody have a quarter?!

SAL, ANGELA, BOB, *and* FEONNA: Ten, nine, eight . . .

GUARD *(to the TOURIST, complete with gestures):* Do you have a quarter for the machine?

(The TOURIST shows his empty pockets.)

SAL, ANGELA, BOB, *and* FEONNA: Seven, six, five . . .

GUARD: Well, this is it, fella. Good-bye.

(He shakes the TOURIST's hand and then hugs him. The TOURIST and the GUARD passionately kiss, while SAL, ANGELA, BOB, and FEONNA shout "Three, two, one!" The lights go out, and everyone screams as a loud crashing sound is heard. The lights come up. The noise from the street that has accompanied the play stops. Everyone is lying on the floor, along with half of a missile that has partially crashed through the ground, taking the TOURIST with it. Nothing remains of the TOURIST except his camera, which lies perfectly intact in front of the missile. There is a long silence.)

ANGELA: What happened?

FEONNA: We must be dead.

GUARD: I don't think the missile detonated.

ANGELA: This is just like every New Year's Eve in Times Square. You spend hours in the cold getting mugged while waiting for this little ball to drop so everyone will know that it's New Year's. And then the little ball drops and everybody acts crazy, but soon you realize that nothing has really changed. It's still cold, and you're still getting mugged.

BOB: Are we still alive?

ANGELA: Yes.

BOB: This is really embarrassing.

GUARD *(looking down through the hole that the missile made):* For one moment I found the love, meaning, and beauty that I had been searching for my whole life. *(BOB looks through the hole.)* Do you think he's dead? *(BOB nods his head.)*

FEONNA: So am I.

ANGELA: You're not dead. *(Looking for SAL.)* SAL! *(She rushes over to him.)*

BOB: I would like to make a donation to the cause to show my strong commitment to peace. *(He takes off his pants and shirt, which are covered with buttons, and hands them to* TANYA. *He then walks inside and makes a phone call.)*

ANGELA *(taking* SAL's *pulse):* He's still alive.

FEONNA: He is?

ANGELA *(opening* SAL's *eyelids):* It's just his brain that's dead. Drug overdose.

GUARD *(crying):* I just can't . . . I don't understand . . . what's the matter with this country? We can't even pull off a successful nuclear war. What will happen to us now?

(BOB opens the door and leans out.)

BOB: Well, good-bye all. I have a meeting in Washington in the morning.

FEONNA: Good-bye, Bob. Oh, did you find out what happened?

BOB: It seems that we sabotaged their missiles and somehow they sabotaged ours. Apparently there was such a high level of infiltration that the KGB was actually the CIA and vice versa. Now I must go to Washington, expose everyone, and become a national hero. *(To* TANYA.*)* I said we would never let a nuclear war occur, and I was right.

ANGELA: What about all that stuff you said about making a mistake and taking responsibility?

BOB: I don't recall making any such statement. Now, enough of this. I must be going, but don't worry, friends, I won't let you down.

(He exits.)

ANGELA *(looking down at* SAL*)*: Well, I guess I'll just bring him back to Astoria, where his mother can take care of him for the rest of his life. *(Looking over the side.)* I hope the car is still there.

FEONNA: Don't go back to Astoria. Why, you can come and live with me. Together we can develop some interests.

TANYA: I guess I have some buttons to sell.

ANGELA: Do you need some help?

GUARD: I'll stay here. After tragedies like this, someone has to clean up.

(FEONNA and ANGELA hold up the buttons and bumper stickers.)

TANYA, FEONNA, *and* ANGELA *(not in unison)*: "Cruise people, not missiles!" Get your buttons and bumper stickers right here! All antinuclear paraphernalia full price!

(Blackout.)

END

CHARLIE SCHULMAN

I am presently a senior at the University of Michigan, where I am a creative writing and literature major and a two-time recipient of the Avery Hopwood Award for Drama. *The Ground Zero Club* is my second play to be produced at the Young Playwrights Festival and was part of the first International Young Playwrights Festival in Sydney, Australia. I am now twenty-one years old (almost twenty-two) and very much an aging Young Playwright. I wrote *The Ground Zero Club* a few years ago and enjoyed the unique experience of having my second play receive a professional production at the age of eighteen. Since then I have been writing plays and short stories while working a part-time job as a rock and roll roadie/stagehand.

WANING CRESCENT MOON
A Play in One Act

BY STEPHEN SERPAS
(age eighteen when play was written)
Baton Rouge, Louisiana

NOTE:
For the purpose of publication in this collection, certain words
have been changed by the playwright and some profanity has
been deleted from the working script of the play as performed at
Playwrights Horizons in New York City, October 6 through 10,
1986.

CHARACTERS

SCOOTER, almost eighteen
HAL, eighteen
GERTIE, forty

A suburb in midwestern America.
The backyard of SCOOTER'S *house.*
Thursday, June 5, 1986.
A midnight of blues and grays, and a feeling of starkness or that the air is dry.

SCOOTER *sits on the grass, surrounded by various objects—a sleeping bag, a few notebooks, a booksack, and a lantern set a few feet away.* HAL, *his best friend, is looking through a telescope, which sits low on a tripod.*

SCOOTER *is gazing into the sky with almost obsessive intensity.*

SCOOTER: Galileo was first. In 1609 he peered through his telescope and saw this massive white in full focus. He was amazed how its surface resembled the earth's.

HAL *(coming up from the telescope):* Scooter . . . I don't see nothing.

SCOOTER: He drew the first map, too. Craters. Mountains. But the large dark areas—he thought they were bodies of water. He called them seas.

HAL: Dark sky. That's all I see.

SCOOTER: You can never see it the same way twice. It runs in a cycle of eight phases and goes through all of them in twenty-nine days.

HAL: Eddie Langford's parents are away for the weekend.

SCOOTER: Are you getting all of this?

HAL: There's going to be a party.

(SCOOTER *looks through the telescope.*)

SCOOTER: The edges are barely distinguishable.

HAL: Brenda's going to be there.

SCOOTER: When it reaches the last quarter, you know there's only a week left.

HAL: Brenda! Brenda 36D Brenda! . . . Scooter—

SCOOTER: Brenda doesn't like me. She dates Eddie.

HAL: I'm not talking about dating, I'm talking about sight-see-ing.

SCOOTER: You know I'm not interested in parties.

HAL: What's to be interested in? It's just a bunch of people hav-ing a good time.

SCOOTER: The social situation. It bores me.

HAL: Come on, man!

SCOOTER: Sorry.

HAL: I should have realized. This is so like you—your attitude.

SCOOTER: If you want to go, go.

HAL: It's not the same deal. You know, when I first found out that you and me were both in Mr. Freeman's astronomy class, I thought it would be a good deal, you know, because we could mess around, do whatever we wanted, you know. Turns out you like this. Look at you, Scooter. Just look. Ever since chapter eight.

SCOOTER: Chapter eight.

HAL: Scooter, I think you're letting them ram this garbage down your throat.

(SCOOTER *continues with his studying, immune to* HAL's *bickering.*)

SCOOTER: The week after the last quarter is spent descending into the last phase. It will reach conjunction with the sun again and disappear.

HAL: Disappear?

SCOOTER: Not exactly. Become unobservable. The visible face will have no sunlight on it. At that point, it is considered new.

HAL: I know who I'm sitting next to for the final. You—you know this.

SCOOTER: Like to think I do.

HAL: Then you can show me this, huh?

SCOOTER: Depends.

HAL: What?

SCOOTER: Are you going to learn it?

HAL: Who, me? Of course, yeah. I know how to be interested in something. I know all of that. I know how to take a test and everything.

SCOOTER: Right, Hal, right. You know how to take a test. Ask anyone who was in Mr. Hamilton's homeroom class last year.

HAL: Last year?

SCOOTER: Big history final.

HAL: Oh, now, come on—

SCOOTER: You had all the multiple choice answers carved into a tree outside the classroom window. Just so happened that you sat right by it.

HAL: They weren't carved. They were meticulously engraved with a cordless wood burner.

SCOOTER: David O'Connor said you'd look out the window pretending like you were gazing—you know, like you were searching your spiritual self for the answers.

HAL: What do you know? Maybe I was just gazing out the window, as if the answers weren't there.

SCOOTER: But they were.

HAL: So—

SCOOTER: Stop lying to yourself.

HAL *(protecting himself)*: David O'Connor's such a jerk, I don't see why you listen to him. I mean, like the time we were in the locker room and we stuffed plastic bags full of motor oil up the shower head so when you turned on the—

SCOOTER: Yeah, yeah, I know.

HAL: He was the one who told Coach Reardon. Three-day suspension.

SCOOTER: You deserved it.

HAL: Oh, come on, man. Joke. You don't really think we'd actually let someone go in there and take a shower, do you?

SCOOTER *(overlapping)*: Yes, I really do think you'd actually let someone go in there and take a shower.

HAL: Well, it didn't work, you remember. Do you know what kind of mess that would—I wonder what kind of shampoo a person would use to get that stuff out?

SCOOTER: If you were so overly concerned with not having any victims, why did you do it in the first place?

HAL: I don't know . . . seemed like the right thing to do at the time. Scooter, man, those gym classes. Boring . . . *stupid* and boring. Jumpin' jacks till your feet fall off. Then you play basketball the rest of the time. And every class is like that all year long. Always seems to rain the very day they get the new archery equipment in. When the weather finally clears up, the archery equipment isn't new anymore. It's broken. Guess someone else got bored, decided to mess with things . . . ticks me off. And you know what really gets to me? I'll tell you: the coaches. I take into consideration that gym class is for fitness, yeah, but what kind of incentive is it to have to look at a forty-two-year-old Schlitz Malt Liquor bull of a physical education teacher? Like, where did they learn to teach this stuff? And they're just sittin' on their can, checkin' out the cheerleaders same as we are. So why don't they pay *us*? . . . I don't know, Scooter. It's a mess, a big mess.

SCOOTER: Gym class.

HAL: Gym class. School. Other things. One big mess.

SCOOTER: Other things?

HAL: Gets so I don't think about stuff anymore.

SCOOTER: Stuff like what?

HAL: Stuff like none of your business, okay?

SCOOTER: Okay.

(SCOOTER *continues with telescope.*)

HAL: It's hard to deal with, that's all.

SCOOTER: What? What is?

HAL: Nothing.

SCOOTER: What, your father?

HAL: No! . . . Yeah . . . I don't know. He tried to hit me again. . . . I don't know, I just don't know. He said I forgot to flush the toilet. How can you argue with him?

SCOOTER: Argue? About flushing the toilet?

HAL: You know—that's how he is. His nature and everything. We could both be on Medicare before the man learns the word *compassion*.

SCOOTER: Just remember, you *have* to live there.

HAL: Yeah. And how is that supposed to make me feel? I feel nothing. I'm like a fifth of whiskey to him—he uses me when he needs me. *(Pause.)* He's not a mental, if that's what you're thinking.

SCOOTER: Does the same go for you?

HAL: Get off it, man.

SCOOTER: Huh?

HAL: Don't start that. Don't start with your analysis routine, because it's getting old, you know? Like ancient history. See, I told you not to read that Freud guy. Now he's going to haunt you for the rest of your life.

SCOOTER: It's not a crime to have an emotion, Hal.

HAL: I know, I'm aware of the situation. It's just—you know.

SCOOTER: I can't believe you.

HAL: Now wait—

SCOOTER: You don't even have the guts to talk about it.

HAL: Now hold on, man!

SCOOTER: Anything. Tell me anything.

HAL: Something's—you're gonna laugh, I know it.

SCOOTER: Just tell me.

HAL: Something's been happening to me. It's like—well, there's like this dream, you know—

SCOOTER: Uh-huh.

HAL: Twice I had it—once three months ago, and then again just last week. I was being chased.

SCOOTER: Uh-huh.

HAL: A big, ugly, three-headed monster.

SCOOTER: You're kidding.

HAL: Purple, green, maybe—I don't know . . . wasn't about to turn around and look. I was running so hard that the veins in my feet came together to form this Styrofoam cushion, this pocket of air that slammed into the earth below me. So what happens next? It chases me into a forest that just appears from nowhere. Thought I was going to have a breakdown or something.

SCOOTER: I see.

HAL: So we're goin' at it, jumpin' through branches, dodgin' trees—the whole bit, you know. After about an hour of running for my life, I trip over a stupid log. Flat on my face. Great. Just great. I'm lying there—broken ankle, something—and I was ready to wet my pants. Curled up like a baby, eyes shut, crying away. I could hear that creature comin', too. Soon enough, he's right in my ear. Mumblin' and moanin' in what sounds like a very primitive form of Spanish. He was hovering above me, and I could feel his heat on the back of my neck. Then it happens. A tap on my shoulder. Then a few seconds. Tap. So I figure, what do I gotta lose? Thing's gonna be gnawing on me one way or another, doesn't really matter what end he starts on. So I take a peek. And never, never in a million years . . .

SCOOTER: What!?

HAL: My dad! It was my dad! He started telling me how he rented the thing from a costume shop and how he'd been planning the whole thing just to make me realize.

SCOOTER: Now that . . . is a dream.

HAL: Dream? It was a nightmare.

SCOOTER: Unbelievable.

HAL: Now do you see what the deal is? Something has to be done. This is not good.

SCOOTER: What are you going to do?

HAL: I've got to get out of here.

SCOOTER: Out of your house.

HAL: Out of the city, maybe.

SCOOTER: Oh, get real!

HAL: I am! Don't doubt me on this, Scooter, because it's gonna happen. Soon. When the right time comes, I'm splittin'.

SCOOTER: Your house is here, your friends, your family—everything.

HAL: What I have ain't a family. It's a good imitation of one, but that's never been good enough. And my dad—he's okay, but he's no Bill Cosby.

SCOOTER: That'd be real stupid to skip town like that. Real stupid.

HAL: Listen to you. You sound like a Boy Scout commercial. "Be prepared. Do things this way. Be responsible." I can't believe you'd let yourself get sucked into that garbage. Where is your danger element? Come on, man!

SCOOTER: Where are you gonna go?

HAL: I don't know. Somewhere.

SCOOTER: You have to find a place to stay, at least.

HAL: I know.

SCOOTER: And food and clothes—

HAL: Thanks, Mom, I understand all that.

SCOOTER: Just wait. You'll see.

HAL: I've got things I'm thinking about.

SCOOTER: So do other people.

HAL: Oh, really?

SCOOTER: Yeah, really.

HAL: Well, that's just great. Just when a person thinks he has friends to depend on. Now this.

SCOOTER: Who, me?

HAL: I was hoping you could help me out.

SCOOTER: What? Money? Hal, I can't—

HAL: No, no, no, no. Just listen.

SCOOTER: Help you out how?

HAL: Listen! I was talking to Eddie Langford. He understands all this, with me and everything. And like, his parents belong to triple A, and he's gonna call them up to map out the trip just as soon as we decide where we're gonna go.

SCOOTER: We? I'm not going anywhere.

HAL: Now listen, just listen. Think about the other day in the cafeteria. I was sitting next to Eddie, Patrick was by you, and we were talking about—you know . . . what's going on.

SCOOTER: What? Oh, no. I was just thinking about that.

HAL: Thinking about thinking of it or thinking about doing it?

SCOOTER: No, Hal.

HAL: Man—

SCOOTER: You really think I could leave right now, think I could pick up and walk away?

HAL: If you're real bummed out here.

SCOOTER: Has nothing to do with it.

HAL: Of course it does.

SCOOTER: Well—

HAL: Are you real bummed out here?

SCOOTER: I don't know.

HAL: What's that mean?

SCOOTER: I just don't know.

HAL: Other day you weren't talking like this. Remember the other day what you were saying?

SCOOTER: I was just mad.

HAL: Didn't mean you didn't mean what you were saying. You said it, didn't you?

SCOOTER: Are you going to keep bugging me about this?

HAL: I'm not bugging you.

SCOOTER: You keep talking about it.

HAL: I'm just trying to help.

SCOOTER: *That* is bugging me.

HAL: Man, what do you want?

SCOOTER: Just stop.

HAL: Seemed clear to me the other day what you were saying—

SCOOTER: *Shut up!*

(Silence.)

HAL: You know, you cheated on your fair share of tests, too, you know. It's not just me. You play around in gym class, I know you do. I know I'm not perfect, but at least I—

SCOOTER: Hal—

HAL: —don't go around pointing the finger. Look at you. Going around saying I'm crazy. You're the one who's truly crazy.

SCOOTER *(remaining stern):* Right.

HAL: I remember the day you were rambling on and on about all that bizarre stuff, thinking you were a prophet of God and everything and how you were going to save the world. You forget—I was there, I saw it. That's how you are when you're off that medication.

SCOOTER *(untouched):* Of course.

HAL: So now this whole control thing you're playing with everyone is just a big joke, man!

SCOOTER *(humoring him):* You're right. That's what it is.

HAL: There's no control. You'd flip out if you didn't have your lithium. It's burned in your blood! To the hilt!

SCOOTER: The miracles of modern medicine.
*(*HAL *laughs at him.)*
Are you finished? Are you satisfied? Come on.

HAL *(slightly embarrassed):* Just testing you. Consider it one of your final exams.

SCOOTER *(trying to speak the truth):* The thing is, I just don't know if I'm ready to turn myself a hundred and eighty degrees right now.

HAL: Not ready?

SCOOTER: I have all these things to deal with here. Look at my mom. And we still haven't heard from my dad.

HAL: What is there to be ready for? Things just happen.

SCOOTER: You don't understand.

HAL: People change for reasons, not because they say they will. Oh, sure. You promise yourself. "I'll do my homework. I'll go to bed early." Rarely do you listen to yourself. I think you change when you need to, and when that happens, it happens in your soul somewhere. You don't realize it.

SCOOTER: What is this, a lecture?

HAL: It's true.

SCOOTER: Okay, okay—suppose it is true. Why? Why worry, why take the chance?

HAL: Hey, man. It's like those coaches say in gym class: "No pain, no gain."

SCOOTER: Think I'll stick with astronomy.

HAL *(a compliment):* You're really into this astronomy thing, aren't you?

SCOOTER: I relate to it.

HAL: Yeah. Maybe if I had taken honors trig, I could really get into it. Guess I'll settle for another D.

(SCOOTER starts to laugh.)
What?

SCOOTER: We really are a couple of jerks, aren't we?

HAL: We are? Yeah, we are.

SCOOTER: I don't know why that's funny. Just is.

HAL: We'll get over it.

SCOOTER: Eventually.

HAL: Hell, it's like with my dad. He chases me around the house with a bat. He doesn't want to hurt me, he just doesn't want me to be a loser. Just wish he'd find a different way to tell me, that's all. That's why I want to take off.

SCOOTER: Yeah.

(They continue to observe the moon. Silence. The porch light snaps on. GERTIE, SCOOTER*'s mother, walks out with a birthday cake, candles flickering in the night. She sings "Happy Birthday" to* SCOOTER, *flashing the cake under his nose.* GERTIE *blows out the candles.)*

GERTIE: And the crowd roars! Hey, you do-do brain! Eat some of this, it's bad for you.

SCOOTER: You're early.

GERTIE: German chocolate. *My* favorite.

SCOOTER: The tenth, Mom. June tenth. You're early.

GERTIE: What's a few days?

SCOOTER: Almost a week.

GERTIE: No big deal.

SCOOTER: Mom—

GERTIE: Okay. We'll celebrate your birthday this week, mine next week.

SCOOTER: You? You're in September.

GERTIE: Okay, when September rolls around, we'll celebrate your father's birthday.

SCOOTER: Ha, ha, see me laughing.

HAL: Hi, Gertie.

GERTIE: Hi, sweetie.

HAL: What's going on?

GERTIE: Routine, routine.

HAL: Keeping busy, huh?

SCOOTER: She prides herself with keeping a full-time job *and* being able to clean the entire house.

HAL: I would. Sounds like a workload.

GERTIE: How's the school business going?

HAL: Talk to Scooter. He's responsible for the both of us.

SCOOTER: The final's tomorrow.

HAL: Guessing would be easier at this point.

GERTIE: Oh, that's lovely.

HAL: Yep. Working hard to protect that old family name. See how good it's working?

SCOOTER: Hal gets preoccupied.

HAL: Scooter *is* preoccupied.

SCOOTER: He never does his homework.

HAL: Who needs to?

SCOOTER: Come on—a D in astronomy?

HAL: So whatta you care?

SCOOTER: I don't. I'm just trying to help.

HAL: So what? You're going to help me by not caring?

SCOOTER: You're getting so defensive.

HAL: Defensive? I'm not getting defensive, you're the one who's—

GERTIE: Why don't you both shut up and let's have some cake?

(Silence.)

HAL: I don't even like astronomy.

SCOOTER: No one asked you to.

GERTIE: Scooter! Cake!

SCOOTER: Okay, okay.

HAL: Good.

SCOOTER: For the moment.

GERTIE: Good. Hal, want a piece?

HAL: I don't think so, I have to get going soon.

GERTIE: Okay. . . . Aw, Gertie, why did you—I completely—it slipped my mind. I don't know how to—

SCOOTER: Something wrong?

GERTIE: Hal, I forgot—your dad called. About an hour ago.

HAL: Oh . . . great.

GERTIE: Honey, I am so sorry.

HAL: No, don't worry—

GERTIE: I was doing the cake and then the oven wouldn't—I had to go to the bathroom and—

HAL: He probably just wants me to—

GERTIE: Hal, really. Tell him it was me. I'll call back and tell him it was me.

HAL: Don't worry. It'll be fine.

GERTIE: Are you sure?

HAL: It'll be okay.

GERTIE: Okay.

HAL *(to* SCOOTER*):* I'm going to go over for a second, check in.

SCOOTER: I'll go with you.

HAL: Really. It's cool.

SCOOTER: What if you need—

HAL: No, I'll just be a minute.

SCOOTER: Okay.

GERTIE: Why don't you take a piece of cake for your dad?

HAL: Oh, I'll get it later. I'm just going to walk over there.

SCOOTER: See you in a little while.

HAL: Sure thing.

*(*HAL *leaves.)*

SCOOTER: I can't believe you did that. Forgot that he called.

GERTIE: It was an accident.

SCOOTER: I still can't believe you did that.

GERTIE: All right already.

SCOOTER: You know what's going to happen.

GERTIE: He said it was okay. What do you think, I did it on purpose?

SCOOTER: No.

GERTIE: Well, then.

SCOOTER: Sorry.

GERTIE: Forget it. How do you like your birthday cake?

SCOOTER: It's not my birthday.

GERTIE: You're so stubborn.

SCOOTER: Probably because of my upbringing.

GERTIE: You, mister, are a nut.

SCOOTER: It's still not my birthday.

GERTIE: So it's a surprise! Get up and dance!

SCOOTER: Why?

GERTIE: Just to do it.

SCOOTER: I don't feel good.

GERTIE: What?

SCOOTER: Mom, I don't see why I have to—

GERTIE: Can't you at least have a piece of this cake? For once in your life stop being so— . . . oh, boy. Rewind. *(Sincerely, with a new beat.)* I didn't mean that.

SCOOTER: You said German chocolate?

(GERTIE *sits beside* SCOOTER.)

GERTIE: You got it, kiddo.

SCOOTER: This is too great. I think I'll drown in it.

GERTIE: Tired?

SCOOTER: A little. Been here since nine.

GERTIE: You're a trooper. Hang in there. *(Offering.)* I was thinking about maybe going shopping for you this weekend. Can you come along?

SCOOTER: Hal and I are going camping, and I have my world history final Monday.

GERTIE: Can you and Hal go camping another weekend?

SCOOTER: Mom, we've been planning this trip for a month, we bought all this food, and I really don't think Hal would—

GERTIE: All right, all right, all right. I just thought that because it's your birthday we could—

SCOOTER: My birthday isn't until Tuesday.

GERTIE: How soon I forget.

SCOOTER: We could go then.

GERTIE: No good. I have to be at the office late. Wednesday?

SCOOTER: Thursday's my English final.

GERTIE: We're real good at this, aren't we?

SCOOTER: It's not my fault.

GERTIE: I didn't say that.

SCOOTER: But you used that tone.

GERTIE: Tone?

SCOOTER: That tone of yours. Irritates me.

GERTIE: What?

SCOOTER: Don't play dumb, you know what I'm talking about.

GERTIE: You're right, I do. So what are we going to do about this birthday of yours?

SCOOTER: Until you brought the cake out, I had forgotten it was even coming up. I mean, I felt that something important was about to happen, but . . . I don't know why. People usually look forward to those things. This time, though, I just . . .

GERTIE: I can't believe you. This from a person who used to raid the closets two weeks ahead of time to see if there were any presents.

SCOOTER: You knew about that?

GERTIE: I have my ways.

SCOOTER: I was just curious.

GERTIE: I know. What happened this time around?

SCOOTER: Other things happening. School. Looking for a job.

GERTIE: Sounds constructive. How, though, are we going to do this?

SCOOTER: Anything's fine. You decide.

GERTIE: Sure?

SCOOTER: Anything.

GERTIE: I was thinking. Near the end of June maybe. Call up all those people you bum around at school with, and I'll give you guys the house for the weekend.

SCOOTER: I don't think so.

GERTIE: What's the problem?

SCOOTER: No problem, I just wouldn't like that.

GERTIE: Why?

SCOOTER: I wouldn't have a good time.

GERTIE: Okay. Maybe we can go someplace. I don't know, someplace.

SCOOTER: Maybe.

GERTIE: You could bring Hal.

SCOOTER: Where would we go?

GERTIE: I'm just throwing out ideas. I don't know.

SCOOTER: Going places—that means spending money, doesn't it?

GERTIE: Usually. Doesn't have to mean spending money.

SCOOTER: Money we don't have.

GERTIE: What do you want me to do, then?

SCOOTER: I don't care.

GERTIE: You said anything.

SCOOTER: I didn't mean anything.

GERTIE: What am I supposed to do!

SCOOTER: Did I ever say you had to do anything for me?

GERTIE: But it's your birthday!

SCOOTER: Are birthday presents going to make things better? A new red fire truck. A piece of cake. Oh, sure that's the answer. How could you think such a thing?

GERTIE: Let's say we forget this, okay? Okay?! "Sure, mom." "Okay, Scooter. Want a piece of cake?" "Yes, I'd like that." "Okay." *(She starts to cut the cake.)* Well . . . *I'm* going to have a piece.

(SCOOTER calms down. He is almost ready to compromise when HAL jogs in.)

HAL: Back again.

GERTIE: Hello.

HAL: Came back for my notebook. Have to be headin' in.

SCOOTER: You didn't bring over a notebook.

HAL: Course I did.

SCOOTER: You said you didn't need it because you were probably going to fail anyway.

HAL: Oh, that's right, that's right.

SCOOTER: What's going on?

HAL: I don't know. He just wants me in.

SCOOTER: But what did he say?

HAL: He said, "Hal, I want you in."

SCOOTER: Is that all?

HAL: Unless you know something I don't.

SCOOTER: Hal—

HAL: What?

SCOOTER: You can tell me.

HAL: What?

SCOOTER: What else happened?

HAL: I don't know what you're talking about.

SCOOTER: Hal, come on . . .

GERTIE: Scooter, leave him alone.

SCOOTER: I can't believe you. Liar.

HAL: Where are you at, man? What is your thing?

GERTIE: He's upset.

HAL: Oh. Hey, Scooter—you know—whatever, you know. Sorry. . . . So what's happening here with the telescope and everything?

SCOOTER: Take a look.

(HAL *looks through the telescope.*)

HAL: I don't know. This is pretty weird.

SCOOTER: What, what's happening? What do you see?

(*They switch places.* SCOOTER *looks.*)

HAL: The very bottom edge. It looks like hair, a giant hair.

GERTIE: What is this?

HAL: The moon does very weird things, Gertie, like things that I don't know about. With shadows, the sun. So we're checkin' it out.

SCOOTER: This is it. Now, if I'm right, we have anywhere from fifteen minutes to an hour.

GERTIE: Hour till what?

HAL: Till the thing happens, you know.

GERTIE: What is it again?

SCOOTER: The moon. It's going to go away for a while. Into another phase. The orbit, of course, stays the same, only we won't be able to see it.

GERTIE: Oh, really? And when did this start to happen?

HAL: Since time began.

GERTIE: I've never noticed that. Or maybe I just assumed it was covered by a cloudy sky. But if it's going to go away, why do you have the telescope out here?

SCOOTER: To see what it looks like before it goes.

HAL: Yeah.

GERTIE: Why?

SCOOTER: To see if anything's different when it comes back. Plus Mr. Freeman's going to give me extra credit for the records I keep of the progression.

GERTIE: Great.

HAL: You never told me that! You never told me he would do that!

SCOOTER: I did, too. Twice I told you.

HAL: When?

SCOOTER: First last Friday during lunch, and yesterday walking home from school.

HAL: You should have told me again.

SCOOTER: Doesn't matter anyway, I think he's only letting *me* do it.

HAL: Why?

SCOOTER: Because it was my idea.

HAL: Right. Now what am I gonna do?

SCOOTER: Why don't you help me?

HAL: What's the use? Scooter, you're so smart, you're such a doormat.

SCOOTER: Only around you, Hal.

GERTIE *(looking into the sky):* I don't see it, where is this?

SCOOTER: Use the telescope.

GERTIE: Ah, I see something. It's the—what is it, the outer edge of it?

SCOOTER: Yes. "The hair," as Hal calls it.

GERTIE: It's so thin. I'm squinting.

SCOOTER: Like I said, it's going away. Taking a vacation.

HAL: Yeah. That's what we can do someday, Scooter. Take a vacation. You know.

(HAL *and* SCOOTER *exchange glances.*)

GERTIE: Nice. You planning on sleeping out here?

SCOOTER: If I need to.

HAL: Don't worry. He'll pick up everything and go *somewhere* with it.

SCOOTER: Yeah. Maybe I'll even go alone.

(*The phone is heard ringing faintly inside the house.* GERTIE *heads for the porch, bringing the cake with her.*)

GERTIE: Be right back.

HAL: Ten dollars, it's for me.

(GERTIE *goes inside.*)

SCOOTER: Thanks, thanks a lot.

HAL: Lay off, man. I got King Kong chasing me through every square inch of a two-story house!

SCOOTER: It's really in your head, isn't it? This hit-the-road thing. Living off of what? A slice of bread a day?

HAL: Man, I'm near the end of it. You just don't know.

SCOOTER: I told you, it's my choice. About all of this.

HAL: Just try and make sure it's the right one, that's all I'm saying.

SCOOTER: And which one is that? The one you want, huh?

HAL: I didn't say that.

SCOOTER: You know, sometimes you're so selfish. It bothers people like you wouldn't believe.

HAL: Oh, so this is what we're getting into.

SCOOTER: Yes, this is exactly what we're getting into.

HAL: Okay then, let's include you in this, too.

SCOOTER: You do that.

HAL: Let's talk about your little fits when you get angry, let's talk about how you manipulate people to feel sorry for you.

SCOOTER: Look who's talking.

HAL: Let's talk about all that garbage. You see? Doesn't feel too good to have another person run down the list on you like that, you just want to walk over and beat the—

(GERTIE *pops her head outside the door.*)

GERTIE: Hal, he wants you home now. And if I were you, I would have left yesterday. (*She goes back in.*)

HAL: Just think, Scooter, think. Different places. Different people. A whole new deal. You just stay here. *Stay here . . .* and think.

(HAL *runs off. Silence.* GERTIE *comes out.*)

GERTIE: That man seemed so pleasant at Sunday barbecues, but now hearing him gaggling over the phone makes me want to pick it right up and get the police to surround the house.

SCOOTER: No, Mom. You know things don't happen like that. And you promised Hal. He has his own way of working this thing out.

GERTIE: That makes me even more anxious.

SCOOTER: Mom, it only happens a few days out of each month, and the most he ever got out of it was a bruise.

GERTIE: A bruise. And that excuses everything, doesn't it? Great. Why don't we just make it an Olympic event?

SCOOTER: Sometimes people are involved in circumstances that are better solved by—

GERTIE: No! In things like this, there are no circumstances, there just *is*!

SCOOTER: No one can even talk to you!

GERTIE: It's his mother's fault. That Margaret. She had to run away with that marketing consultant from Minnesota and fly off to Mexico somewhere . . .

SCOOTER: How can you—

GERTIE: . . . the nerve.

SCOOTER: Oh, come on—Margo's only part of the reason. You don't know the half of it.

GERTIE: I know I have a responsibility to a family. I have a kid to bring up. It's nice to get away for a while, but what she did? To think! I used to have coffee and cigarettes with that lady . . . can't get over it.

SCOOTER: Well, go ahead, write her off completely.

GERTIE: Hey, don't think *we're* ahead of many people.

SCOOTER: Oh, so now everyone else on the block is better off.

GERTIE: Some of them are.

SCOOTER: Some of them.

GERTIE: Some more than others. Wait till school gets out, then everyone will be in a state of panic. All those rich people who use school to get rid of their kids'll realize that they are responsible for another human being. That's when they get nervous.

SCOOTER: Yeah, but it only lasts a few days until the applications for summer camp are in. Then they ship them off somewhere else.

GERTIE: Convenient for them, I'm sure. *(Complaining.)* I can't *believe* some people . . . if we were in another country or something, things like that would never happen. I read somewhere that families in Russia are very close and always together.

SCOOTER: Of course. Where are they gonna go?

GERTIE: Look at China. They live their lives through a philosophy. That man, Confucius, he was no deadbeat.

SCOOTER: Now, there's something misleading: the Chinese and their proverbs. Here's a country with all this profound knowledge, yet they haven't figured out a way to help all the starving people living there.

GERTIE: Now you're just rationalizing.

SCOOTER: Of course. I have to do something to make my point. I'm not gonna sit here and let you show me up.

GERTIE: Is that so?

SCOOTER: My mom smarter than me? We're talking major embarrassment.

GERTIE *(laughs a bit):* You're such a nut! Some of the things you say . . . How are you feeling, baby?

SCOOTER: Fine.

GERTIE: You're not tired or anything?

SCOOTER: Little sweaty. I'm going to take a shower.

GERTIE: Can I get you something? Water?

SCOOTER: No, thanks.

GERTIE: You gonna start taking it easy?

SCOOTER: Yes.

GERTIE: Get all the rest you need now.

SCOOTER: I will. Hal and I are going to have a big weekend. Going camping and all.

GERTIE: That's not what I meant.

SCOOTER: I know what you meant. *(Pause.)* Do we always have to end up talking about this?

GERTIE: No.

SCOOTER: So why does it always happen?

GERTIE: It's not my fault.

SCOOTER: I didn't say that.

GERTIE: You asked me like it was my fault.

SCOOTER: Sorry.

GERTIE: I *would* like to ask you something. How come every time we *do* talk about it, you think I'm putting you down or trying to get inside you or searching for something I don't know about?

SCOOTER: What?

GERTIE: You always do something with your face or get that whiny sound in your voice whenever I mention it.

SCOOTER: Great, thanks a lot.

GERTIE: See, that's what I mean. That whiny sound.

SCOOTER: Whiny sound? This is just my voice.

GERTIE: Your voice being whiny.

SCOOTER: What can I do about it? Or if you want to make this really difficult, what can you do about it?

GERTIE: I hate it. I hate it when you make me fight you.

SCOOTER: Then don't.

GERTIE: Crazy. It's just crazy. I mean, the circumstances that we jump into each day are—

SCOOTER: Circumstances. I thought there were none—there just is, remember?

GERTIE: Okay. You got me. You win.

SCOOTER: Win? Win what? Another one of our petty arguments over ways to fix my brain?

GERTIE: Not this again.

SCOOTER: Isn't that why I'm being drugged until I start seeing two of everything?

GERTIE: You don't even want to help yourself, do you?

SCOOTER: Is there really a way? I'd like to know how. Oh, come on. You're there with the doctor, you're standing there next to me. "Scooter, just remain strong these next couple of months, and you'll be fine." He didn't even offer me an original statement.

Just some contrived remark to help my feet walk out of that place for the twentieth time. Help myself? I don't even want to *be* myself.

GERTIE: I don't understand you. Why do you want to stop living your life again? That's what you're saying to me, am I right? This time around you have a choice. You're choosing *no*. Do you really intend to make this another stop? Because I'm starting to wonder how many of these we're going to make. Now, in theory, we can make as many as we want and still get through this thing, but from my arrogant point of view, all of these stops are slowing us down. *(More motherlike.)* Scooter, you've gotta snap out of this. This bitterness you have inside you. Can't you see yourself? I mean, would it make sense to punish your lungs by refusing to breathe? Please.

(Silence.)

SCOOTER: You know, it's hereditary.

GERTIE: What?

SCOOTER: That's what Dr. Henry said. It's hereditary. Generations of our family had and will have this blessed disease.

GERTIE: It's not a disease.

SCOOTER: Excuse me. Chemical imbalance. Through every hall of Northdale High School you can see Scooter Ashmore, walking quietly, keeping to himself. And about ten feet behind him are two to three sophomore girls who possess an annoying giggle quality. "Is he the one?" "Yeah. Basket case. So-and-so told me. He's the one." *(Pause.)* There's no dignity in this. No honor. How do you explain why you were out of school for three months? I tell them I broke my leg or something? Right. The truth? Then what? Strange looks, false sympathy. "There, there —it'll be okay." I feel like a lost animal that the whole world found on the street. *(Simply.)* I don't want people accommodating for me. I just want to be who I was. And you wonder why I don't want to have a party with all those people I bum around at school with. And Hal's trying to drag me off to some weekend beer bash over at Eddie's house. I'm surrounded by people who think there's an easy solution to all of this.

GERTIE: Scooter, the kids at school don't mean anything when they—

SCOOTER: The kids at school are children. So there.

GERTIE: Well, how do you ever expect them to understand if you keep filling the space between the two of you?

SCOOTER: I don't know!

GERTIE: Then think, Scooter, think! You're the one trying to convince us all that you can function as well as anyone else. So find a way!

SCOOTER: I'm trying!

GERTIE: Try harder!

SCOOTER *(defenseless):* I mean, I really am trying. . . . Mom, what's happening to me?

GERTIE: A little inconvenience, Scooter. That's all. *(Recalls, trying to empathize.)* I *do* remember what Dr. Henry said. What a voice he has. How he mumbles. Mumbles like a doctor. Writes like a doctor. You get the prescription, and it looks like a printing of your biorhythm.

SCOOTER: Dad hated him.

GERTIE: I knew he hated him. It was the hospital itself, mostly. The stark whiteness of the place gave him the shakes.

SCOOTER: He would shake?

GERTIE: Always. As long as I've known him. He was hit-and-miss putting the ring on my finger.

SCOOTER: Was it a chemical thing or something?

GERTIE: Psychological overload. You know, worried too much, smoked too much.

SCOOTER: Yeah.

GERTIE: Bills to pay, or it's the "job." Oh, honey, it's the "job."

SCOOTER: I never noticed that.

GERTIE: All the time. Things would pile up, and his hands were like butterflies. At the hospital anyway—I knew he was uncomfortable being there, but he knew it was something he had to do.

SCOOTER: He said this to you?

GERTIE: No, I just knew.

SCOOTER: How?

GERTIE: I don't know. I guess the same way I know about his shakes. Being around a person for nineteen years, you know what he's saying even when he's not talking.

SCOOTER: And this is what he "said" to you?

GERTIE: At the time.

SCOOTER: At the time. What about the middle of November, what was he saying to you then?

GERTIE: Scooter—

SCOOTER: I'd really like to hear his reasons for taking off the way he did.

GERTIE: I told you once before.

SCOOTER: I want to hear it again, though.

GERTIE: I don't feel like I have to explain anything. Your father was a good man—that's all. His reasons were his own. It was something he had to do for himself. How could I have stopped him?

SCOOTER: I can't believe you accept that. I can't believe you live with that. He skips off to who-knows-where with some woman that you and I have never seen before, and you're saying it's okay. Did you ever check anyplace? Did you ever try and find him?

GERTIE: He'll be back one day.

SCOOTER: Who are you kidding? He's done a fantastic job at lying to the both of us. Last summer, all I could think about was the trip to Hawaii we were going to make in November. I should have known.

GERTIE: How could we? You were in the hospital for three months.

SCOOTER: And he's been gone twice that long. Was he so anxious that he couldn't wait up for me?

GERTIE: How was he supposed to know when you'd get out?

SCOOTER: I bet you that's where he is now. Stretched out over the entire beach. Showing himself he can have a good time without us.

GERTIE: It's not that at all.

SCOOTER: Then I suppose you know, huh? I suppose you know the who, what, and why about the whole situation, don't you? Don't try to explain what's clear to me. We're living off the weekly pay of a receptionist, we eat like gerbils, and one of us cannot allow stress to make us sick again. I don't see how you've developed this attitude.

GERTIE: Attitude?

SCOOTER: That things are just gonna blow over, and then we'll return to where we started.

GERTIE: I'm just trying to hold on to what we have.

SCOOTER: Then what's this about you couldn't've stopped him or you don't feel like you have to explain anything? Am I not a part of this? Should I have to keep guessing? Because I feel awful, you know that. I feel embarrassed and confused and tired. And everyone wants to know what it is that makes me crazy. *This is it.* People hiding the truth from me—that's what makes me crazy. Did you hear what I said? Does that make any sense to you? . . . It's getting really hard to pass your room at night. You crying the way you do. It frightens me.

GERTIE: And so you eavesdrop on me now. Is that what's happening?

SCOOTER: It's hardly a matter of eavesdropping unless one directs full attention to the art of crying privately.

GERTIE: Maybe, but that's not—the point is if you would have just— You have some nerve, boy!

SCOOTER: If I would have just not cared.

GERTIE: You are being so damned selfish about this! It's me that's on the line for all of this. Me! So do me a favor—be the child. Enough with this "You've developed an attitude" number. Just don't think about financial obligation or where your next meal is coming from. Darren took the car and the whole thirty-four hundred dollars that was to be your first year of college! *Now* tell me what else you need me to explain!

(SCOOTER *turns away and thumbs through a book.*)

GERTIE *(pseudoparental):* Look at me, son, when I'm talking to you.

(SCOOTER *does not answer.*)

Scooter Michael—*(Nothing.)* Oh, so you're just going to thumb through that book. Is that it? Pretend like nothing's happening. Brilliant. Studying hard so you can grow up to be something great. Grow up to marry someone who can give you the type of kids that possess a burning desire to look through telescopes. All these manically depressed children running around with lunar computer read-outs. Yeah, that's where you see everything, don't you? Everything's preset and focused through that one tiny hole. Well, if it works so well, why don't you use it to view something you hardly ever see—me? Use it to see me, Scooter. To see me. Listen to me! I'm right here! Among all these things. Right here, right here! You're supposed to see me, that's all. To see me.

SCOOTER *(without maudlin):* I do see you . . . it just hurts so much to look. *(Faces her fully.)* Why did dad leave you?

GERTIE: For that lady, Clara. The one he met at the country club.

SCOOTER: Yeah, that's what you told me before, but I want to hear the truth now.

GERTIE: I'm telling you the truth.

SCOOTER: Was he given an offer he couldn't refuse?

GERTIE: He said it would be a while before he got back in touch with me.

SCOOTER: And you didn't want to move because you love this house so much?

GERTIE: Six months of child support is what he owes us.

SCOOTER: Or maybe he was involved in organized crime, and the cops were closing in on him.

GERTIE: With that kind of money, you might be able to go to school in the fall.

SCOOTER: Was there any particular reason he decided to disassociate with us?

GERTIE: I'm sure there are many colleges in the Midwest that have telescopes beyond your wildest dreams.

SCOOTER: Can you think of a particular reason?

GERTIE: I don't understand you.

SCOOTER: Maybe there was a person he was having problems with.

GERTIE: Please tell me that you're not talking like this.

SCOOTER: Can you think of anybody he might of ran into problems with?

GERTIE: It was the shock of the whole thing that hit him, not just the—

SCOOTER: Huh?

GERTIE: What I mean is, he was—

SCOOTER: What? What was he?

GERTIE: Oh, Scooter!

SCOOTER: He was "oh, Scooter," is that what he was?

GERTIE: No!

SCOOTER: Well then, you're going to have to clarify what you're talking about because all of this mumbling is—

GERTIE: HE LEFT BECAUSE OF YOU, ALL RIGHT? HE LEFT BECAUSE OF YOUR BLESSED DISEASE! You little bastard, he left me all alone . . . *(Breathes slower.)* One night he told me that a mental health ward was not the place for his only child to be. It was not what he intended at all. There was no big good-bye. Just a note explaining about the house and everything and some money. I burned the note. The couple of hundred dollars he left—well, you always said you wanted to look at the stars. *(Disgruntled.)* Look at me, though. It's taken six months. Six months to realize all of this.

SCOOTER: It's okay.

GERTIE: Never thought your mom would turn out to be such a jerk, did you?

SCOOTER: It would take too much energy to think something like that.

GERTIE: I really wouldn't blame you if you hated me.

SCOOTER *(laughs weakly):* For what? Telling me something I wanted to know, something that I already knew? I should hate myself. *(Secretively.)* Since I left the place, I didn't know how I should feel. First there was "What happened to Dad?" And then there was "How am I going to catch up in school?" There wasn't time to look back. You knew I tried to talk with you about it. Thousands of times. Clammed up, every time. Then I figured it out. It's kinda hard to cry "Mommy" if it's going to make your mommy cry harder than you. But how else was I going to find out? I didn't know! *(Mad at himself.)* What a dumb thing for me to do! Getting sick. What a dumb thing!

GERTIE: No, baby, stop yourself. Don't say it that way. Don't.

SCOOTER: Yeah, I know, I know. I'm sorry. *(He catches his breath.)* So what am I gonna do?

GERTIE: Do what you have to do.

SCOOTER: Yeah. *(Pause.)* Mom . . . I've got to leave this place.

GERTIE: I know.

SCOOTER: I mean, I've *got* to leave this place.

GERTIE: When?

SCOOTER: Soon. Very soon. A couple of weeks. Hal and I.

GERTIE: What a pair.

SCOOTER: It'll work out.

GERTIE *(more intimate):* What's going to be different for you? What's going to change?

SCOOTER: People will see *me.* I'll be considered new.

(She kisses and hugs him. They share a moment of observing each other. She finally breaks the moment: letting go. She walks to the porch.)

GERTIE: Don't forget to turn off the porch light when you're finished.

(She goes inside. SCOOTER *takes a moment to make sense of all this. Then he goes back to the telescope to continue observations. Long pause.* HAL *quietly sneaks into the yard.)*

HAL *(whispering):* Scooter!

SCOOTER *(turning):* What the—? Why are you back?

HAL *(running to him):* I jumped out my bedroom window. He's probably drunk to the floor by now. *(Points to telescope.)* What's going on, what's happening with this thing?

SCOOTER: Let's see. *(He looks, makes a small adjustment.)* There.

HAL: What's the deal?

SCOOTER: It's like three or four grains of salt against a blackboard.

HAL: What?

SCOOTER: The last phase. The waning crescent of the moon.

HAL: Well, get out the way, let me see.

(They switch places. HAL *looks.)*
Hey . . . hey! I don't see nothing, Scooter. The thing up and left on me.

SCOOTER: Guess you weren't quick enough.

HAL: Hey, Scooter.

SCOOTER: Yeah?

HAL: Bite the big one.

SCOOTER *(laughs):* Don't worry. There'll be other times.

HAL: Yeah, right.

SCOOTER: I . . . I told my mom that I'm leaving. I told her you and I are going to hit the road together.

HAL: You—! You did this! I can't believe it!

SCOOTER: Right before you came over.

HAL: Scooter, my man, yes! We are going—this—there are gonna be some good times ahead of us, you know what I'm saying!

SCOOTER: I know, Hal, I know.

HAL: I can't believe it!

SCOOTER: Just one thing, Hal, one thing.

HAL: What's that?

SCOOTER *(handing him a book):* Graduation.

HAL *(taking book):* Oh . . . that's right.

(They start to study.)

HAL: Scooter?

SCOOTER: Hmmm?

HAL: If we ever end up getting an apartment or something like that, can we keep all the books in your room?

SCOOTER: Yes, Hal.

HAL: Good.

(They resume studying.)

STEPHEN SERPAS

Like my peers, I was fortunate enough to attend a high school that excelled in the performing arts. At Baton Rouge High School I studied singing, drama, and musical theater. My senior year of high school, my first play, *Plastic People,* was produced by my advanced play production class. It was taken to the Festival of New Works at the Contemporary Arts Center in New Orleans, where it won first prize. From there I went to Chicago and studied acting at the Goodman School of Drama for one year. I have written four more one-act plays and several scenes and monologues. *Waning Crescent Moon* is my third play. I have been an associate member of The Dramatists Guild for three years. I am currently majoring in dramatic writing at the Tisch School of the Arts, part of New York University.

NOTES ON THE PLAY

The most valuable thing I have learned from participating in the Festival is the evolution—the process—that a script actually goes through before presentation.

Waning Crescent Moon focuses on the idea of change and how it can help you as much as it scares you. During the year the play was under the helmet of the Festival, and when it came back to me for revisions was a helpful, exciting, and—yes—scary time.

The first draft contained a good portion of what you have in your hands now. Gone, though, are the huge thematic arias of what I thought the play should be. I've learned that overwriting stems from a writer thinking, "Will they get it?" Most of the time the answer is yes. You can always take away from what is there, the important thing is to *have* something there.

Under the guidance of my collaborators, later drafts went

through a more difficult test. Is this word needed? Is this line adding to character or plot revelation? Is the rhythm being sustained without sacrificing clarity? Questions I never even considered came up, and I had to have the answers. That, however, is the challenge of the playwright. To make everything work within a production so that it still has your voice but also serves the needs of the director and actors. That dirty word *compromise* comes to mind. I think it is a fine thing to do if it's going to improve what is there. If it works, keep it.

For its initial reading, Director Don Scardino and Dramaturg Richard Greenberg brought out the emotional steps the piece needed to reach its climax. Over the summer came a cut-and-paste session, letting more phrases balance on the unspoken word. In a larger context, Director Thomas Babe and Dramaturg Sybille Pearson examined the work on a true professional level and expected true professional results. I am grateful to all of them for their interest and ability.

Perhaps what is painful about writing is that, most of the time, you end up cutting your favorite line or monologue. It teaches you not to fall in love with your words and to think in more unified terms. It is disappointing all the same.

One thing I confronted myself with during the rehearsal process: "Is all of this really worth my time?" After going through the process and seeing it with an audience and knowing that my play communicates, I know it definitely is.

REMEDIAL ENGLISH

BY EVAN SMITH
(age eighteen when play was written)
Savannah, Georgia

NOTE:
For the purpose of publication in this collection, certain words
have been changed by the playwright and some profanity has
been deleted from the working script of the play as performed at
Playwrights Horizons in New York City, September 16 through
October 12, 1986.

CHARACTERS

VINCENT RYAN
SISTER BEATRICE
ROB ANDREWS
CHRIS
DAVID
COACH

SCENE ONE

The setting: Cabrini Catholic Academy, a private high school for boys in a medium-size southern city; and VINCENT's *home.*
The time: One day of school, and that evening.
The rising curtain reveals VINCENT *and* SISTER BEATRICE *alone onstage.* VINCENT *is seated right, and* SISTER BEATRICE *is seated behind a desk, left.*

   VINCENT *is wearing the Cabrini Catholic Academy uniform of a blue knit sportshirt with the school crest over the left breast, khaki slacks, a black belt, and black penny loafers. He is in the waiting room of the office of* SISTER BEATRICE, *a teaching nun. She is, however, a post–Vatican II nun; she is wearing, not a flowing black habit and wimple, but a navy blue skirt, a white blouse buttoned to the neck, nurse's shoes, and a shapeless polyester blazer of white and light blue stripes. On the jacket lapel is a simple stainless-steel cross. At present, she is fully occupied grading test papers, and* VINCENT *is fully occupied waiting. In fact, the expression on his face as the curtain rises is enough to imply that he has been waiting for quite some time.*

   VINCENT *leans forward in his chair as if to look through a half-open door into* SISTER BEATRICE's *office. All he sees is* SISTER *gleefully wielding a red pen. He leans back, stretches, and then addresses her. She cannot hear what is essentially an interior monologue.*

VINCENT: Sister, I think it's very rude of you to keep me waiting like this. It's been fifteen minutes since you said, "I'll be finished in a minute," and unless I'm doing worse in algebra than I thought, you're off by fourteen minutes. Fourteen minutes may not seem like much to you—time moves pretty quickly after your hundredth birthday—but this is *supposed* to be my study hall. I have many important things to do during my study hall. I am developing a fascinating abstract pattern to fill the margins of my chemistry book; I'm right in the middle of *Lake Wobegon Days;* and I have almost finished my project of inserting the complete works of Judith Krantz into the library's card catalog. This is a school, after all, Sister. You of all people shouldn't want to see me wasting my time.

What did I do to merit such treatment? Is it because of that little tiff we had in English yesterday? Sister, we all say things in the heat of argument that we later regret. I'm sorry I called T. S. Eliot a "social-climbing Yankee papist." I don't even remember what I *meant* by that!

Have you forgotten all the good times we have had together? Don't you remember Dramatic Literature, when I was a sophomore? We read aloud to the class . . . I was Jean . . . you were Miss Julie . . .

Oh, good grief, *please* don't tell me you found the Sister Beatrice Virgin Vote! God, how could I ever explain that? But if you *did* find it, you should at least be pleased with the results! Fifty-eight percent of my music class said that they thought you were a virgin. Sister, you've got to understand—such a large part of my life is spent in your company, and yet I hardly know anything about you! You've got to expect a certain amount of healthy curiosity and speculation. Do you ever wish you hadn't become a nun? What would you have done instead? Do you have any regrets? *Are* you a . . . Never any answers from this woman of mystery. Oh, well, you take your time, Sister, I don't mind waiting.

(VINCENT returns to his seat. SISTER appears to be finishing up her work. She shuffles her paper into order, looks at her watch, and goes to the unseen door.)

SISTER: There. I thought I'd never finish these. Thank you for waiting so patiently.

VINCENT: You know what a patient disposition I have, Sister. But I must admit, I am rather shocked to see you spending your mornings hurriedly finishing up work from the night before. I was always told to do my homework at home.

SISTER: I expect you to do as I say, not as I do. Besides, this is a Monday morning, my least favorite of the week, and these are from D-Group. You'll notice I used up three red pens.

VINCENT: Ah, D-Group. That's the class that laughs every time you mention a dangling participle.

SISTER: Perhaps, perhaps. But they have their good points, too. For example, they never contradict me, unlike certain young men. There is something very charming about a class that believes everything you say.

VINCENT: Now, that wouldn't be any fun. Your mind would rot.

SISTER: Speaking of mind-rot, I've been looking over your transcript.

VINCENT: Sister, it's a perfectly respectable transcript.

SISTER: Well, well, let's see. Shall we examine it more closely?

VINCENT: Do we have to?

SISTER: Now, your standardized test scores put you in the ninety-ninth percentile.

VINCENT: That's good.

SISTER: Yes, that's very good. It would lead one to believe that you were an intelligent young man.

VINCENT *(Mr. Humility):* Well . . .

SISTER: But we know better.

VINCENT: We do?

SISTER: Of course. Because we come down here, and we see that your grade-point average is a C.

VINCENT: A very high C! Five one-hundredths from a B.

SISTER: It was enough to keep you out of the Honor Society.

VINCENT: I know.

SISTER: Vincent, there is no excuse for a student of your ability to be making such grades.

VINCENT: I have an A in your class, Sister.

SISTER: And what about algebra? And history? And Christian morality?

VINCENT: Now, sometimes I pay a lot of attention in that class.

SISTER: I'm not talking about waking up long enough to proclaim the death of God and then going back to sleep! Getting attention from you in class is like drawing blood from a stone. You're a million miles away every day. You have a mind! Why don't you use it?

VINCENT: I do! Remember all those "Beetle Baileys" I translated into Latin?

SISTER: That's very admirable.

VINCENT: Thank you.

SISTER: I am the last person to throw cold water on a young man's creativity. But the point I am trying to make is that you don't give everything equal access to that mind of yours. And so, Mr. Ryan, we come to the purpose of this little chat.

VINCENT: You mean there's more?

SISTER: Oh, yes! As you know, I have a class of D-Group students, all of whom are bright and eager to learn.

VINCENT: Despite the fact that they haven't quite gotten the knack of their opposable thumbs.

SISTER (*after giving him a short, disapproving smile*): As it turns out, some of them want so desperately to learn that I have decided they should have personal tutors.

VINCENT: Are they failing that badly?

SISTER: Worse. But they need senior English to graduate, and the last thing I want is Mommy calling me up to ask why I am keeping her little Johnny from graduating with his friends.

VINCENT: What has this got to do with me? I'm not failing anything.

SISTER: It occurred to me that the best way to bring you down from your little cloud would be to give you a student of your own. You are going to be an English tutor.

VINCENT: You're going to make a problem student a tutor?

SISTER: I want you to know what it's like to talk yourself blue in the face to a blank wall. So for one hour every day, sometime after school, you will teach English to one of my D-Group students. Now, I was thinking of giving you Bubba Thompson. . . .

VINCENT: Uh, Bubba Thompson. Gee, I don't think so . . .

SISTER: What do you mean?

VINCENT: Well, we had cross words once, and I don't think we would get along very well.

SISTER: You had cross words with Bubba Thompson?

VINCENT: Well, I had cross words, and he just furrowed his brow and tried to understand what I was saying.

SISTER: I see. Well, who have we got?

VINCENT *(hesitatingly):* What about, um, Rob Andrews?

(ROB enters from left and goes to his locker. A young man of VINCENT's age, ROB is drop-dead beautiful. He is wearing old shorts, shoes, and shirt for PE. He opens his locker, which contains his school uniform, and takes off his shirt.)

He's in that class, isn't he?

SISTER *(checking her list):* Yes, he is. And he isn't doing any better than anyone else. Why? Would you rather tutor him?

VINCENT *(thinking quickly):* Oh, well, it's just that I kind of know him from PE. Our lockers are across from each other.

(ROB by now has taken off his shoes and socks, and he now takes off his shorts, revealing white cotton briefs. He stretches, and is apparently reluctant to put his uniform on.)
We've become pretty good friends.

SISTER: Oh, well, that will never do. I can't have you tutoring your best friend; you wouldn't get anything done.

VINCENT: Oh, no, no, no! We're not *best* friends. We're more like nodding acquaintances. You know, we just sort of know each other. We only have one real class together, history, and so we kind of know who the other person is; that way, we wouldn't be going into this strangers. We could get right to work.

(ROB has gotten his uniform out of his locker and put on his shirt.)

SISTER: Well, then, that's fine with me. You will be paid five dollars an hour.

VINCENT: Great.

SISTER: And I'll tell Mr. Andrews.

VINCENT: Fine.

SISTER: Now, you've really got to make an effort to teach him.

VINCENT: Oh, I will.

SISTER: Because he needs to pass to graduate.

VINCENT: I understand.

(ROB *has got his pants on.*)

SISTER: So if that is all—

(SISTER *freezes for* VINCENT'*s next speech.*)

VINCENT: Uh, Sister, I do think I should tell you that the only reason I finagled my way into tutoring Rob Andrews is because he is the best-looking boy I have ever seen in my life, and I have been obsessed by him ever since we were freshmen. And the only way I know him from PE is I watch him change his clothes every chance I get. In actuality, I know him about as well as I know Mary Tyler Moore.

(ROB *has now got his school shoes on and his PE clothes put away.* SISTER *returns to normal.*)

SISTER: You've got a class shortly.

VINCENT: That's right.

SISTER: And this is your first day of tutoring.

VINCENT: Oh, really? I didn't realize.

SISTER: Yes, today. Don't forget.

VINCENT: I won't. 'Bye.

SISTER: Good-bye, now.

VINCENT: Uh, Sister, if you don't mind my asking, what did you do before you became a nun?

SISTER: I became a novice right after I graduated from high school. Why?

VINCENT: Just curious. Thank you. 'Bye.

SISTER: Good-bye.

(He leaves her office, then stops center stage.)

VINCENT: Virgin.

SCENE TWO

(The lights fade on SISTER *as* ROB *finishes dressing and moves center.* ROB *and* VINCENT *meet.)*

VINCENT: Looks like I'm going to be your tutor.

ROB: Yep.

VINCENT: So, like, when do you want to meet? After school?

ROB: Can't. Gotta work. How about eight?

VINCENT: Fine.

ROB: Where?

VINCENT: Uh—my house?

ROB: Okay. But I gotta leave by nine.

VINCENT: Perfect.

ROB: Yeah.

VINCENT: So I'll see you at eight, then. . . .

ROB: Sure.

VINCENT: Hey, have we got history next?

ROB: Uh, yeah, we do.

VINCENT: I guess I'd better get my book, then!

ROB: Yeah.

VINCENT: Well, I'll be seeing you. . . .

ROB: Sure.

(ROB exits, and VINCENT watches him. After he is gone, VINCENT stands a moment, then collapses in a heap.)

SCENE THREE

(Lights come up on the history classroom. There are five desks. They contain VINCENT, CHRIS, DAVID, *and* ROB. *There is one empty desk. Behind his desk sits the* COACH.)

COACH *(disinterested and poorly informed):* And so, gentlemen, the uh, Greeks wound up going from pretty much Athens in the west, to uh, pretty much Persia and, uh, almost India in the east, which was pretty darned big in those days. And all this was pretty much the fault of Alexander the Great.

*(*CHRIS *raises his hand.)*
Uh, yes, Christopher, what may I do for you, sir?

CHRIS: Wasn't Alexander the Great a homosexual?

(The class laughs, except VINCENT *and* CHRIS, *who knows he can get away with this by playing it straight.)*

COACH: Well, Chris, are you looking for a role model or something?

CHRIS: No, no. I'm just trying to find out the whole story. I'm really into history, you know?

COACH: Yeah, I know. You're trying to be a jackass is what.

CHRIS: No, really, Coach, isn't that true? Wasn't Alexander the Great a little light in the loafers?

COACH: I'll be perfectly honest with you, I haven't got the slightest idea. But we are not here to discuss the, uh, questionable personal habits of historical figures. Now if you'll be so kind as to let me continue?

CHRIS: Oh, sure, Coach.

COACH: Thank you.

CHRIS: Anytime.

(COACH *gives him a look that says "Shut up," and* CHRIS *laughs.*)

COACH: As I was saying, the Greek Empire went from Athens to Persia, and the Greeks kind of spread their culture all over that area in between. It was called, I believe, Hellenic culture, and you might want to write that down, gentlemen. I don't think your memories are all that good, expecially going by your last tests . . .

(*The* COACH's *voice begins to fade, and the lights focus on* VINCENT.)

VINCENT: Rob is really the most beautiful boy I have ever seen in real life. And when you think about it, being beautiful is as good as being smart, or athletic, or a really great singer. All of those things you're born with, so what makes being born smart better than being born beautiful? Everybody is born with a *most:* most beautiful, most talented, or, for that matter, most obnoxious. I hope my *most* is a good one.

(*As soon as* COACH *speaks, the lights come back up, and* VINCENT *is taken by surprise.*)

COACH: So, Mr. Ryan, what do you suppose the answer to that question might be?

VINCENT: Well, Coach, I've been giving that one some thought, and you know, I'm really stumped. That's a tough one.

COACH: Yeah, it is. The answer, gentlemen, is Sparta, the most militant of the Greek city-states. Now, if you guys think that this school is strict, you would've wet your pants in Sparta. . . .

CHRIS: Coach, if the Greeks were so tough, how did the Romans kick their ass?

COACH: That's a good question, Chris. . . .

(Once again, the COACH *becomes silent as the lights focus on* VIN-CENT.*)*

VINCENT: Chris is just bubbling over with *mosts.* I mean, he's just a great guy. He plays football and basketball both very well, and if his plays don't always make the team win, boy, do they make him look good. He's handsome, too. If you don't believe me, just ask him. And he's so smart! Gets straight A's. He spends every night before a test studying his voluminous notes, and sometimes he changes those voluminous notes into little tiny notes. And sometimes he keeps on studying those little tiny notes right up to and during the test! What dedication!

DAVID: Coach, how could the Romans and the Greeks both have Asia Minor in their empires? I thought they were enemies.

CHRIS: Because they didn't have them at the same time! Look at the dates on the maps, you idiot!

*(*CHRIS *leans far over in his desk to bop* DAVID *on the head with his book.)*

DAVID: Ow!

CHRIS: Sorry about that, Coach. You've gotta discipline him, or he'll never learn.

VINCENT: David here is smart, but he tries too hard. If he would only calm down long enough to use his brain, he would have something to offer the world. He and Chris became friends in kindergarten over twelve years ago, and they've forgotten how not to be. They are best friends out of habit. In the same way, David is part of the group: out of habit. But if he were to walk into class today, not knowing a soul, I wouldn't give him one semester. On the other hand, he could surprise you. He has a very resilient ego.

*(*VINCENT *goes over to* ROB's *desk and kneels beside it.)*

And then there is Rob, who is . . . beautiful.

(VINCENT becomes lost in reverie.)

COACH: Mr. Ryan.

(Slowly VINCENT returns to his desk.)
Mr. Ryan.

(VINCENT sits.)
Vincent, are you there, sir?

(The lights return to normal. VINCENT looks up as the class laughs.)
Uh, would you like to tell us what was going on in there, Mr. Ryan? Or should I just mark you absent today?

VINCENT: Oh, you don't have to do that, Coach.

COACH: I don't. I feel like I should thank you or something. If you don't start paying more attention, I'll thank you with this stapler upside your head. Now, Chris, why don't you tell us what was so all-fired special about the way the Greeks ran their outer provinces.

CHRIS: Sure, Coach. Well, the Greeks didn't like to bring in a bunch of their own guys to run a conquered territory, so they just kept the local people and pretty much let them keep their own laws, too, not like the Romans who . . .

(As CHRIS's voice fades, so do the lights. VINCENT is still staring at ROB.)

SCENE FOUR

(Lights come up on VINCENT *alone, center stage.)*

VINCENT: The Cabrini Catholic Academy handbook is very clear on what is considered proper behavior in the halls. A student has exactly three minutes to get from class to class, during which time he is to conduct himself in a manner befitting an institution of learning; ergo, there is to be no running, no eating, no talking, and no roughhousing. However, if you want to talk, go ahead, that one is never enforced. Or better yet, sing. At the top of your lungs. Only one song, however, is considered proper for hall-singing:

*(*VINCENT *begins singing to an Army marching tune.)*

"Two old ladies lyin' in bed
One roll over and the other one said,
I wanna be an Airborne Ranger!"

Under no circumstances should you be caught singing "Over the Rainbow." As a general rule of thumb, any Judy Garland tune is out. If you find the official Cabrini bookbag too cumbersome, there is a world of variety in the way you can carry your books. There is this—

(in his right hand)
and there is this—

(in his left hand)
Never carry your books like this—

(across his chest)

All of these rules, of course, are widely disregarded. But you never know who is watching.

(VINCENT *looks carefully to the left, then to the right, then sings a few lines of a torch song in the style of a Forties crooner. He is transported to Carnegie Hall. He bows as the lights fade.)*

SCENE FIVE

(Lights up on the English room. VINCENT, DAVID, *and* CHRIS *are sitting with expressions of mixed amusement, morbid curiosity, and disbelief;* SISTER BEATRICE *is reciting.)*

SISTER: "Hear the sledges with the bells—
Silver bells!
What a world of merriment their melody foretells!
How they tinkle, tinkle, tinkle
In the icy air of night!
While the stars that oversprinkle
All the heavens, seem to twinkle
With a crystalline delight!
Keeping time, time, time,
In a sort of Runic rhyme,
To the tintinnabulation that so musically wells,
From the bells, bells, bells, bells,
Bells, bells, bells—
From the jingling and the tinkling of the bells.

. . .

Hear the loud alarum bells—
Brazen bells!
What a tale of terror, now, their turbulency tells!
In the startled ear of night
How they scream out their affright!
Too much horrified to speak
They can only shriek! shriek!
Out of tune,
In a clamorous appealing to the mercy of the fire,
In a mad expostulation with the deaf and frantic fire,
. . .
By the sinking and the swelling in the anger of the bells—
. . .
Of the bells, bells, bells, bells,
Bells, bells, bells—
In the clamor and the clangor of the bells!

Hear the tolling of the bells,
Iron bells!
What a world of solemn thought their monody compels!
In the silence of the night
How we shiver with affright
At the melancholy menace of their tone!
For every sound that floats
From the rust within their throats
Is a groan!
. . .
To the tolling of the bells,
Of the bells, bells, bells, bells,
Bells, bells, bells!
To the moaning and the groaning of the bells!"

(She throws herself into a deep curtsy, then bounces up, very pleased with her performance.)
That was "The Bells" by Edgar Allan Poe. David, suppose you tell us what the chief poetic device of this poem is.

DAVID: Huh?! Well, uh . . .

(DAVID immediately becomes flustered and searches vainly through his book for the answer.)

I've got the answer right here. . . .

SISTER: Christopher, why don't you help him out?

CHRIS: Well—

DAVID: No, I know this one. I know it! *(His search continues fruitlessly.)*

SISTER: Christopher?

CHRIS: As I was saying, *personification* is . . .

DAVID *(having finally found the answer):* Personification!

(DAVID *gives up disgustedly.*)

CHRIS: . . . the chief poetic device of this poem, "The Bells," by Edgar Allan Poe. A very fine poem, I might add.

SISTER: I'm glad you think so, Christopher. Why don't you tell us what it says to you?

(CHRIS *does far better with one-word answers. He pauses. He has never, however, been one to let ignorance keep him from voicing an opinion, so he forges ahead.*)

CHRIS: Well, this poem told me a lot about bells. I felt I really got to know the different kinds and their individual qualities—I especially enjoyed the part about the alarum bells, I could really feel the danger in the air.

SISTER: Very good, Christopher. Mr. Ryan, what did you think of "The Bells"?

VINCENT: Um, it had some interesting images. . . .

SISTER: Interesting images.

VINCENT: Some nice word-play . . .

SISTER: Word-play.

VINCENT: Very evocative descriptions . . .

SISTER: Good descriptions. What else?

VINCENT: To be perfectly honest—

SISTER: What?

VINCENT: It is the silliest poem I have ever read.

SISTER: Since you are so enthusiastic about "The Bells," class, why don't you write a simple thousand-word essay discussing the author's purpose in writing it?

CHRIS: But Sister! I *do* like it!

SISTER: Then you shouldn't mind writing about it.

CHRIS *(more to* VINCENT *than to* SISTER*):* *I* didn't say it was silly.

SISTER: Right now we will go on to our next poem, since we're almost out of time. On page 232, you will find "A Noiseless, Patient Spider" by Walt Whitman.

DAVID: Wasn't he a homo?

SISTER: Be quiet, David.

(She takes a deep breath, opens her mouth, and is about to speak when the class-change bell rings. CHRIS *and* DAVID *fly out, leaving* VINCENT *and a disappointed* SISTER BEATRICE*.)*

VINCENT: Hear the lunch bell, joyful bell.

SISTER: Never make fun of a woman when she's down.

VINCENT: Are you down?

SISTER: Have you ever felt that you're spending your entire life trying to make a point that nobody gets?

VINCENT: You would be surprised, Sister.

SISTER: Your day is coming, young man. Have you spoken to Mr. Andrews?

VINCENT: Yes, this morning.

SISTER: You will soon know exactly what I'm talking about.

VINCENT: Oh, you are too smart for me, Sister.

SISTER: You have to get up pretty early, Mr. Ryan. Pretty early.

VINCENT: Sister knows best.

(SISTER has her papers together and is about to leave the room.)

SISTER: And by the way, when you are tutoring Mr. Andrews, keep your mind on English.

VINCENT: I beg your pardon?

SISTER: Your mind is so susceptible to wandering. Keep it on English, understand? 'Bye.

(SISTER exits, and VINCENT looks after her thoughtfully.)

SCENE SIX

(Lights come up on the lunchroom. At a table sit CHRIS, VINCENT, *and* DAVID. *They are eating their lunches.)*

CHRIS: Geez, David, sometimes you are such an idiot! The tangent wave begins at negative one-half pi, not zero; when you're drawing the phase shift, you start at negative one-half pi, not zero. When you draw the phase shift for sine or cosine, then you begin at zero!

DAVID: But I thought Mrs. Allen said—

CHRIS: Will you forget what you thought Mrs. Allen said? You never think right anyway. For Pete's sake, you're usually half asleep in that class anyway. No wonder you're failing.

DAVID: I'm not failing.

CHRIS: Oh, excuse me, you've got a D minus, that's such a big difference!

DAVID: Well, it's not failing.

CHRIS: You will be failing after the test tomorrow; I can see you getting a twelve.

DAVID: The only reason you're passing is because you cheat all the time.

CHRIS: *You* cheat! But you still fail! You're the only person I know who can cheat on a test and still get a forty-four. *(To* VINCENT.) You know what he did? He had all the answers to the multiple choice in code on his pencil, but this idiot starts at the wrong end of his pencil and fills them all in backward! You're just lucky Mrs. Allen didn't realize that if she had graded your paper backward, you would have had a hundred. Geez, you're stupid!

DAVID: Vincent, what did you get?

VINCENT: What?

DAVID: In algebra and trig?

VINCENT: Oh, an eighty-two.

CHRIS: I got a ninety-eight.

VINCENT: Yeah, but I got an honest eighty-two. An eighty-two to be proud of. An eighty-two that says, "Hey, I learned eighty-two percent of this chapter." Your ninety-eight says, "Chris can cheat without getting caught."

CHRIS: That's an accomplishment, too.

VINCENT: I thought we were in school to learn.

CHRIS: Learn? Here? Ha! We're in high school to get practice in faking our way through life.

DAVID: And to party.

CHRIS: And to party! *Party!* I think I can safely say I have fully learned the art of partying. All you need is three kegs and a hundred people.

DAVID: And a good band.

CHRIS: Right. Aw, hell. You know what I heard? They're gonna get the same band for the prom this year that they had last year. That sucks.

DAVID: Yeah, well . . . Who are you taking?

CHRIS: Patricia. Who are you taking?

DAVID: You know who I'm taking.

CHRIS: Sharon?! You're actually taking Sharon?

DAVID: What's wrong with that? I like Sharon.

CHRIS: Why? Does she fetch? Can she play dead?

DAVID: Very funny.

CHRIS: Does she have a sister? Or should I say a litter? We could fix Vincent up—

VINCENT: Leave David alone. He should be able to attend the prom with the date of his choice, free from harassment.

CHRIS: Who are you taking?

VINCENT: Me?

CHRIS: Yeah, who?

VINCENT *(after a pause):* I don't dance.

CHRIS: You can't get a date?

DAVID: You don't have to dance.

VINCENT: I can get a date.

CHRIS: Who are you gonna ask?

VINCENT: I don't know.

CHRIS: Yeah.

(The lights focus on VINCENT.*)*
Sharon. David, you are a jerk.

VINCENT: Actually, Chris, I was thinking of asking Rob Andrews.

DAVID: Would you just forget it?

VINCENT: I think we would look pretty sharp together, in evening wear.

CHRIS: How can I? I have to be seen with you.

VINCENT: I can't dance, though. Of course, he could lead. . . .

DAVID: You don't even know her!

VINCENT: I've never asked someone for a date before; I don't know how. . . .

CHRIS: I hope to keep it that way.

VINCENT: Rob in a tuxedo . . .

DAVID: There's more to a girl than just being pretty.

VINCENT: We'd go to dinner afterward. I guess I'd have to pay.

CHRIS: I've noticed. That's what makes them such bitches.

VINCENT: I'd say good-bye to him on his front porch. . . .

DAVID: You've got to have a better reason for wanting to spend time with a girl than just she's good-looking. Don't you agree, Vincent?

(Lights snap back to normal.)

VINCENT: Yeah! What?

DAVID: Shouldn't you have a better reason for going with a girl than just she's beautiful?

VINCENT: Absolutely.

CHRIS: What would you know?

VINCENT: What I lack in experience I make up in moral fortitude. A girl's physical attractions should be the last of her qualities put under consideration.

(As VINCENT *finishes that little pontification,* ROB *enters from the right and crosses to the left.* VINCENT *sees him, feels terribly hypocritical, puts his head on the table, and covers his face.)*
Oh . . .

*(*CHRIS, *meanwhile, stops* ROB.*)*

CHRIS: Rob, what time is it?

ROB: Five after one.

CHRIS: Yo, wait up. The bell is about to ring; wake up, guy. You'll be late.

*(*VINCENT *sheepishly picks up his head.)*

VINCENT *(to* ROB*):* Hello.

ROB: Hi.

VINCENT: Haven't forgotten about tonight?

ROB: Nope. Eight.

VINCENT: Eight.

*(*ROB *and* DAVID *exit.)*

CHRIS: What's at eight?

VINCENT: I'm going to tutor Rob in English.

CHRIS: You're going to tutor Rob Andrews?

VINCENT: Yeah.

CHRIS: Ha! Good luck!

VINCENT: Why, thank you, Chris. Maybe I will get lucky.

SCENE SEVEN

(Lights come up in the locker room. VINCENT *has his PE clothes in a bag.)*

VINCENT: It is interesting to note, I believe, that fidelity is responsible for the making of more saints than the apparition of Mary and the Stigmata combined. Among favorite plot devices in opera, fidelity is second only to the intercepted letter and is way ahead of the babe kidnapped at birth. It is my belief, however, that both Bernadette and Butterfly would break under the weight of maintaining fidelity of thought in the Cabrini locker room; especially to a jock who had difficulty remembering their names. Nonetheless, I am the picture of nonchalance and self-control in the locker room. The jock of my dreams is wearing nothing more than a towel as he walks by me? I'd rather hear about David Gray's sister's braces; very complex orthodontal tools, those. The finest butt in the school is walking back from the shower stark naked? I wouldn't notice such a thing; I'm too busy trying to repair a badly frayed shoelace. *(He pulls out a tennis shoe.)* You can't let these things go on too long. You could wind up with serious sneaker damage.

*(*DAVID *enters and sits down on the bench in front of the locker next to* VINCENT. ROB *enters left and exits right, gym bag in hand.* DAVID *and* VINCENT *begin to change for PE, starting with their shoes and socks.)*

DAVID: I'm not failing, and he knows I'm not. I've got a seventy-four, and if I get anything higher than an eighty-nine on this next test, it will be a seventy-five, and that's a C. Of course, if I get anything lower than a forty, I'll have a sixty-nine, which *is* failing, but I'm not worried about that. The only reason I got that forty-four was because of the term paper in global perspectives—I didn't have any time to study. I'll probably wind up with a C, or if I really work, I could have a B. But I'm not failing. Chris is the one who had better watch out about failing. One of these days, he's gonna get caught cheating, and then see if he's president of the Math Club!

VINCENT: Why are you telling me all this? Tell Chris. You shouldn't let him talk to you the way he does.

DAVID: Nah, then I'd never hear the end of it.

(There is a pause.)

You know, Miz Culbert caught him cheating once, but she didn't do anything. She just took his test. If I got caught cheating, I would be put on suspension so fast, it wouldn't even be funny.

VINCENT: No, you wouldn't, and neither would I. We're too well liked by the faculty.

DAVID: You know, Miz Culbert would be pretty, but her tits are too small.

VINCENT: What?

DAVID: Miz Culbert's tits are too small. She would be pretty, but she's got no chest.

VINCENT: Are you serious?

DAVID: Yeah, haven't you ever noticed?

VINCENT: No, I can't say that I have.

DAVID: Really? How could you help it?

VINCENT: I just don't notice that kind of thing.

DAVID: That's weird, man.

VINCENT: It's not weird. Why is that weird?

DAVID: I don't know. That's all I think about in music. What about Miss Sanders? Have you ever noticed her chest?

VINCENT *(exasperated)*: David, you've known me for three years, can't you—

(There is an awkward pause. VINCENT *is afraid to finish what he has begun, and* DAVID *doesn't often see* VINCENT *upset. Then, from offstage, we hear* CHRIS's *voice, followed shortly by* CHRIS.)

CHRIS: "Two old ladies lyin' in bed!

(He appears.)

One roll over and the other one said,

(He hits DAVID *on the head with a football.)*

I wanna be an Airborne Ranger!"

(To DAVID.) Come on, man, you're on my team today. Vincent, think fast! *(He throws the football at* VINCENT *and exits.)*

DAVID: Are you going to play today?

VINCENT: I don't think so.

*(*DAVID *exits. Lights up on* VINCENT, *center, tossing the football in one hand.)*

VINCENT: I've grown to like PE. I'm not much into sports, but then the coaches aren't much into getting me into sports. So I just pretend like I'm participating, and they pretend like they don't know I'm pretending. It works out very nicely; they can concentrate on coaching the guys who are actually interested in football, and I can concentrate on the guys. Well, really, one guy in particular. It's a purely academic interest, mind you—after all, I have only a scant five hours to prepare for an evening tutorial.

SCENE EIGHT

(The lights come up on the living room of VINCENT*'s house. There is a sofa center.* VINCENT *tries on clothes to find the right look. Suddenly, he hears a silent doorbell ring. He goes to the door, and opens it, revealing* ROB. *They fall into a passionate kiss. Then* VINCENT, *still embraced by* ROB, *pulls his head back and looks at the other boy.)*

VINCENT: Sure you're gonna do that.

(He pushes ROB *out the door. He starts to pace, occasionally looking at his watch. Then he sits down. The doorbell really rings.* VINCENT *opens the door, and* ROB *enters, dressed in a jacket, a tank-top T-shirt and jeans. He carries a textbook, a notebook, and a pen.)*

Well, hello. Come in.

ROB: Hi.

VINCENT: Did you just get off work?

ROB: No, I had to go home and shower first.

VINCENT: Oh, I see.

ROB: Why, am I late?

VINCENT: Only about forty minutes. I hadn't really noticed until now.

ROB: I'm sorry.

VINCENT: Don't worry about it, but we don't have a whole lot of time left. Didn't you say you had to be somewhere at nine?

ROB: Yeah.

VINCENT: So . . . have a seat. (VINCENT *notices that* ROB *is already seated.*) How are you doing in English? Sister Beatrice made it sound like you were having some trouble.

ROB: I guess you could say that.

VINCENT: What are your grades like?

ROB: Mostly failing. But I did get a C the other day.

VINCENT: Well, that's . . . average, at least.

ROB: Yeah.

(There is a pause.)

VINCENT: What are y'all studying right now?

ROB: English.

VINCENT: Yes, but, uh, what aspect of English?

ROB: Oh, we're in poetry right now.

VINCENT: Yeah, she's got my class on the same thing. Does she read to y'all?

ROB: Yeah.

VINCENT: She's quite a character, sometimes.

ROB: Yeah.

(Pause.)

VINCENT: Is that your book?

ROB: Yeah, it is. Here.

(ROB *hands the book to* VINCENT.)

VINCENT: What page are y'all on?

ROB: 547.

(VINCENT *finds the page.*)

VINCENT: Ah, "There Is No Frigate Like a Book." Have you read this?

ROB: Maybe, I don't remember.

VINCENT: Oh. Okay. I'll read it.

"There is no frigate like a book
  To take us lands away,
Nor any coursers like a page
  Of prancing poetry.
This traverse may the poorest take
  Without oppress of toll;
How frugal is the chariot
  That bears the human soul!"

Um, did you notice how the words she chose enhanced the meaning of the poem?

ROB: What was the meaning?

VINCENT: Well, what do you think?

ROB: I don't know, we haven't gone over that one yet. Sometimes she gives us stuff to read and never does tell us what it means.

VINCENT: Yeah, she does that to us, too.

ROB: But she expects us to know it for a test.

VINCENT: Oh, well, that's her way. . . .

ROB: She's a bitch, that's all.

VINCENT: Well, be that as it may, when Emily Dickinson wrote "There Is No . . ."—

ROB: What was her name?

VINCENT: Emily Dickinson.

(ROB gets out his pen and starts to write in his notebook.)

ROB: Dick—in—son. . . . Wasn't she the bitch who lived locked away in her house all her life?

VINCENT: Uh, yes, but I wouldn't exactly call her a bitch.

ROB: You know what I mean. It doesn't sound like she was completely normal.

VINCENT: Nobody is.

ROB: Whatever. So what does it mean? *(He is poised to take notes.)*

VINCENT: She is just saying that books are a way of traveling around the world in your mind, that doesn't cost anything, and—

ROB: Wait!

(ROB is writing laboriously. VINCENT is amazed to find that he is taking down his every word)

. . . doesn't . . . cost . . . anything . . . and. What now?

VINCENT: I guess that pretty much says it.

ROB: Great. What's next?

(ROB smiles; apparently poetry is going to be easier than he thought.)

VINCENT: Um, well, let's see. *(He looks at the next page.)* It's "On Going to the Wars" by Richard Lovelace.

ROB: Like in Linda?

VINCENT: I suppose so, yeah. It goes like this:

"Tell me not, Sweet, I am unkind
  That from the nunnery
Of thy chaste breast and quiet mind,
  To war and arms I fly.

True, a new mistress now I chase,
  The first foe in the field;
And with a stronger faith embrace
  A sword, a horse, a shield.

Yet this inconstancy is such
  As you, too, shall adore;
I could not love thee, Dear, so much,
  Loved I not honor more."

This poem always gets on my nerves.

(ROB starts to write this down.)

No, no, you don't have to write that. I'll tell you when you should write something down. I was just going to say that my personal opinion of the poem is that it is highly irritating, not to mention philosophically unsound.

ROB: Why's that?

VINCENT: Well, here's this guy telling his girlfriend he's going to risk his life for honor. That's stupid; he's probably fighting over hunting rights in some royal forest, and he'll probably come out without a scratch while a couple hundred of his serfs will be hacked to death—in the name of honor. Wars aren't fought for noble reasons; they're fought over money. I can't think of any war worth fighting.

ROB: Well, what if the Russians invaded us, what then?

VINCENT: If they want the country that badly, let them have it.

ROB: That's stupid.

VINCENT: No, think. Communism and dictatorship will never take hold in America. Russia's known nothing but tyranny for the past thousand years. We've had freedom since the sixteen hundreds. We'd never stand for it; it just wouldn't work.

ROB: So we would have to fight them.

VINCENT: No, we could use peaceful methods like civil disobedience or passive resistance. Haven't you ever heard of Gandhi?

ROB: The guy in the movie?

VINCENT: Yeah. He freed India from the English without fighting a war.

ROB: Oh.

VINCENT: Yeah!

ROB: Well, I still think we should nuke 'em off the face of the earth.

VINCENT: That is the most asinine statement I have ever heard in my life.

ROB: Oh? What does *asinine* mean? *(He takes off his jacket to reveal a tight tank-top T-shirt.)*

VINCENT: Asinine means . . . interesting; that is the most . . . interesting statement I have ever heard in my life. That brings us to "Oh Who Is That Young Sinner" by A. E. Housman.

ROB: Hey, are we almost done? 'Cause I've got to meet my girlfriend soon.

(Pause.)

VINCENT: Girlfriend?

ROB: Yeah.

(Pause.)

VINCENT: Oh, who is it—she! Who is she?

ROB: Joan McNamara.

VINCENT: Oh, I know Joan! Does she still drive that pink Volkswagen?

ROB: No, she totaled it.

VINCENT: Wow, was she hurt?

ROB: No. But her father had to relay the foundation of their pool.

VINCENT: Oh . . . heh, that sounds like Joan. Ya'll are supposed to go out tonight?

ROB: Yeah.

VINCENT: Gonna get something to eat?

ROB: Maybe. Might just hang out at her house. But, hey, don't think I won't have any time to study.

VINCENT: No, no. I wasn't even thinking about that. Just being nosy, I guess. I don't go out much.

(There is a pause.)
But anyway. Our next poem is "The Garden of Love" by William Blake.

ROB: Sounds like a porno flick.

VINCENT: "I went to the Garden of Love
And saw what I never had seen.
A chapel was built in the midst,
Where I used to play on the green.

And the gates of the chapel were shut,
And 'Thou Shalt Not' writ over the door;
So I turned to the Garden of Love
That so many sweet flowers bore;

And I saw it was filled with graves
And tombstones where flowers should be;
And priests in black gowns were walking their rounds
And binding with briars my joys and desires."

So you see that the Garden of Love is really a metaphor for organized religion. He is saying that the "Thou Shalt Not" approach to religion takes most of the innocent fun out of life. It's binding with briars his joys and desires. (VINCENT *takes a deep breath.*) And I really doubt he was thinking of this when he wrote the poem, but I can't help but associate that last line with—homosexuality.

ROB: You mean this poem is about fags?

VINCENT: No! I mean . . . it could be, if you wanted to see it that way. I mean, uh, it fits in with the general idea, in that homosexuals don't really hurt anyone, and yet most of organized religion is screaming at them that they are sinners, when all they are doing is having sex, and what's so awful about that?

ROB: When it's two guys? That's sick.

VINCENT: Maybe to you, but not to them, so why is it your business? Why is it the Church's business?

ROB: It's in the Bible.

VINCENT: A lot of things are in the Bible! In the Old Testament it says not to eat ham, do you follow that? In the New Testament, it says to forgive your enemies, to turn the other cheek, an idea the Old Testament totally contradicts. Do you know that in grade school, the nuns told me it was all right to kill during a war? That God wouldn't mind?

ROB: That's true. It's okay when there's a war on.

VINCENT: Not if you follow the teachings of Christ. And I have yet to meet a Christian who does.

ROB: You're a Christian.

VINCENT: Not really. I'm an atheist.

ROB: You are not.

VINCENT: Yes, I am. Is that hard to believe?

ROB: You're really an atheist?

VINCENT: Sure. My belief about God is that there is none. Jews don't accept Christ. Well, I don't accept any of it.

ROB: You've got some strange ideas, man.

VINCENT: What, that I think that if two people love each other, they should be able to have sex, be it man-man, woman-woman, or even man-woman? That it's wrong to kill people wholesale over something stupid like oil lanes, or land, or worse still, politics? That Christ should be taken at His meaning, not at His word? Those ideas aren't strange at all. In fact, the poets have been screaming all of that at the pigheaded human race ever since time began! If you ask me, to believe anything else is not only strange but dangerous!

(There is a short pause as VINCENT *exults in self-righteousness.)*

ROB: Should I be takin' notes or something?

(That takes all the wind out of VINCENT. *He slumps down onto the sofa.)*

VINCENT: No.

ROB: Okay. *(He looks at his watch.)* Hey, I've gotta be going. *(He gathers his books.)* It's been real interesting.

VINCENT: Really interesting. It's been really interesting.

ROB: Oh. Sure. So, uh, will I see you tomorrow night, same time?

*(*ROB *freezes.)*

VINCENT: Tomorrow night, same time? You mean forty minutes late? What nerve! Sister Beatrice meant this to be a challenge, but I'm not up to it! He calls Emily Dickinson a bitch, can't figure out "There Is No Frigate Like a Book," and is a warmonger to boot! I don't care how beautiful he is, if he tries to walk through that door tomorrow night, I'll clobber him with the family Bible!

ROB: Will I see you tomorrow night, same time?

VINCENT: Sure.

ROB: Great. Well, I've gotta be going. See ya.

*(*ROB *is at the door.)*

VINCENT: Wait! *(Lightly.)* Do you feel like you've learned anything tonight?

ROB *(enthusiastically):* Yeah! I've got that Dickinson bitch down cold.

VINCENT: Oh. Well, that's great.

ROB: See ya.

(ROB exits. VINCENT stands a moment in thought. He then crosses to the mirror in which he looked at himself at the beginning of the scene, and looks again. He looks away, then crosses to the sofa, where he picks up ROB's English book and distractedly thumbs through the pages. Then he remembers something. He looks up a certain page in the book and reads aloud.)

VINCENT: "Oh, life is a glorious cycle of song,
A medley of extemporanea;
And love is a thing that can never go wrong;
And I am Marie of Roumania."

(Lights fade to black.)

EVAN SMITH

"I've got to go home. I'm writing this play to enter in this contest, and it has to be in the mail tomorrow, and I haven't even begun to type it."

"I'm going back to Savannah. Yeah, I know three weeks is a short time, but I'm sure that art school isn't for me. Maybe I'll be a writer. I'm waiting to hear from this contest. . . ."

"I'll know definitely by March, but I'm sure I won't win. The play is godawful."

"What do you mean, someone from the Young Playwrights Festival called?! Where was I? Why didn't you get me?! My God, don't you realize what this means?!"

"Well, the guy who played Matthew Broderick's best friend in *Ferris Bueller's Day Off* was gonna do it, but he got offered this movie. Yeah, that's what I said."

"I've been trying to think of something for the ending."

"What do you think of this for the ending?"

"I have an idea for the ending."

"Well, it's too late to worry about that now."

"Oh, I've been a big fan of yours ever since I got the album of *Sweeney Todd.*"

"John Simon surprised me, too."

"I've already missed a week of winter quarter, but anyway, good luck with next year's contest. 'Bye."

"No, it wasn't done on Broadway. It was Off Broadway. It's kind of hard to explain, but I did meet some pretty important people. I met Stephen Sondheim. What? Oh, well, he writes musicals, you see. Have you ever heard that song, 'Send in the Clowns'?"

"Whadda they mean, *The Ground Zero Club and Other Plays*"?